PROVING GOD©

PROVING GOD

Dr. Sandra G. Kennedy

Proving God by Dr. Sandra G. Kennedy
Published by *Sandra Kennedy Ministries, Inc.*
2621 Washington Rd.
Augusta, GA 30904
www.SandraKennedy.org

Unless otherwise noted, all Scripture quotations are from the King James Version of the Bible.

Design Director: Bill Johnson
Cover design by Terry Clifton

Visit the author's website: www.SandraKennedy.org

Library of Congress Cataloging-in-Publication Data: 2012952864
International Standard Book Number: 978-0-9788286-7-7

First edition

13 14 15 16 17 — 9 8 7 6 5 4 3 2 1
Printed in the United States of America

TABLE *of* CONTENTS

Chapter 1
PROVE HIM!

DO YOU BELIEVE that God is trustworthy and that He is who He says He is? Do you believe God's Word is true and that He is faithful to His Word? Did you know that God actually wants us to "prove" His Word? Well, He does! God wants us to come before Him and present our case based on what He has said in His Word. That's proving His Word. That's proving God! The very notion that God can be proven is a powerful concept that can change your life. It can change a person's perception of God from being a theological entity to a real, living, powerful, personal God who has a heart for His people, a heart to bring blessings and transformation. This principle—proving God—can change a life, a family, a church. I've seen this not only in my own life, but in the lives of others and in our church. Glory to God!

> But test and prove all things [until you can recognize] what is good; [to that] hold fast.
>
> —1 THESSALONIANS 5:21, AMP

We find in the Bible that not only *can* we prove God, but that God actually *wants* us to prove Him and prove His Word. In Malachi 3:8–10, the Lord says to the people:

> Will a man rob God? Yet ye have robbed me. But ye say, Wherein have we robbed thee? In tithes and offerings. Ye are cursed with a curse: for ye have robbed me, even this whole nation. Bring ye all the

> tithes into the storehouse, that there may be meat in mine house, *and prove me now herewith, saith the Lord of hosts*, if I will not open you the windows of heaven, and pour you out a blessing, that there shall not be room enough to receive it (emphasis added).

"Prove Me," God says. "Prove Me." God's not saying, "Try Me." He's not saying, "Experiment with Me." He is simply saying, "Prove Me." I believe we're living in a time when we need to prove God. We need to give God room to show us what a mighty God He is. In these days, there are many skeptics, even in the Church. They go to church week in and week out for years and years, not really expecting God to do anything. They go to church and then go home and are just the same as when they went. And they don't challenge God to do anything. And guess what? Nothing happens. They get what they expected. Nothing! In their minds, it's OK not to expect anything from God, much less prove God. But God wants His people to expect Him to do great things. He wants us to challenge Him to prove Himself mighty, true and faithful!

It is evident from the Bible that God wants us to come to Him and hold His Word up to Him. He says, "Come now, and let us reason together" (Isaiah 1:18). God is not only willing to hear what we have to say but He wants us to justify our expectations and give a reason why we expect what we expect from Him based on His own words.

In Isaiah 41:21 God makes it very clear that He wants us to present our case to Him, to present evidence of why we can expect Him to do what we have asked of Him.

> Produce your cause, saith the LORD; bring forth your strong reasons...
>
> —ISAIAH 41:21

> "Present your case," the LORD says. "Bring forward your strong arguments..."
>
> —ISAIAH 41:21, NAS

> I am the Lord, the King of Israel, Come argue your case with me. Present your evidence...
>
> —ISAIAH 41:21, CEV

God not only says for us to come reason with Him and lay out our expectations, but He has also told us to bring back to His remembrance what He has promised:

> Put me in remembrance: let us plead together: declare thou, that thou mayest be justified.
>
> —ISAIAH 43:26

"Put me in remembrance." God is telling us to put Him in remembrance of His Word. The question is, can we do that? Do we know His Word well enough to put Him in remembrance of it? Do we know enough of God's Word in order to present our case before Him? He is saying to us, "Come and present your case. State your cause. Come tell Me what you need from Me and why I should grant it. Come tell Me why you should be healed. Come tell Me why you should be delivered. Come tell Me why you should be walking in prosperity." In other words, God says, "Find it in My Word, then bring it to My remembrance."

God doesn't tell us to put Him in remembrance because He has forgotten His Word; He tells us because He wants to see if we know what His Word actually says. God is saying to us, "Come talk to Me. Present your strong argument, your strong reasons. Declare, speak up so you may be justified. Let's reason together. Show Me in My Word why your marriage should be like Heaven on earth, why you should be more than a conqueror, why you can rest in Me. Tell Me why you know you don't have to worry or be anxious. Come tell Me why you should be living above that situation and not beneath it. Tell Me why you expect Me to take care of you, guard and protect you." "Prove Me," says the Lord. "Prove that My Word is true. Prove that I am faithful to My Word." God is looking for His people to come to Him and say, "I have been bought by the Blood of Jesus. I am Your Child, Lord. I belong to You. I serve You. I worship You. I honor You. I thank You for Your Holy Spirit that lives in me. I am a vessel of honor to serve and worship You. Lord, I come to You boldly and I praise You for the answer. I'm standing on what You said, Lord. I don't care what anyone else says. I'm standing on Your Word."

God is your Healer, the One that takes sickness and disease from your bodies (Exodus 23:25). Prove Him. Say to Him, "Lord, You said that You sent Your Word and healed me (Psalm 107:20) and that by Your stripes I am healed (Isaiah 53:5, 1 Peter 2:24); therefore, no matter what the doctor says, no matter what my body feels like, no matter what the symptoms are, I stand firm on Your Word and declare that I am healed." Then watch God prove Himself. God is obligated because of His character and His nature to carry out His Word and bring forth the manifestation of it in your life because God and His Word are one and the same.

When God says, "What do you want? What do you need?

Come present your case to Me," what are you supposed to do? If you are born again, washed in the blood of Jesus, and have found a promise of God that relates to you, then you have the right to come boldly to the throne of God and find help in your time of need. If you need a job, finances, a home, a car, healing, deliverance, or anything that requires God's intervention…then you have a right to go in as His child and expect Him to meet that need!

Chapter 2

THEY HAD BEEN WITH JESUS

THE BIBLE IS full of accounts of people that took God at His Word, then placed a demand on that Word and actually proved God was true and faithful. For instance, Acts 4:1–13 recounts the incident where Peter and John, being filled with the Holy Ghost, began to boldly proclaim the power of God. Think about this amazing incident. Peter and John were going to the temple. They encountered a man who was lame from birth. Peter spoke to him in the Name of Jesus, took him by the hand, and the man leaped up, totally healed and restored. Then all the people began praising and glorifying God. The Bible says the people who witnessed this miracle "marveled and were in amazement." Peter questioned why the people marveled. They were looking at Peter and John as though they had done this by their own power. Peter boldly proclaimed the power of God. He explained that it was not him but Jesus, the Son of God, who had performed the miracle. Peter and John spoke so confidently that the religious leaders were irate because the people listened and believed them. They even had them arrested for teaching about Jesus. The next day Peter and John were brought out to be publicly questioned. The religious leaders wanted to know by what power, name, or authority they had healed a crippled man. Peter boldly proclaimed that the miracle he performed was in and by the power of the Name of Jesus.

> And as they spake unto the people, the priests, and the captain of the temple, and the Sadducees, came

upon them, Being grieved that they taught the people, and preached through Jesus the resurrection from the dead. And they laid hands on them, and put them in hold unto the next day: for it was now eventide. Howbeit many of them which heard the word believed; and the number of the men was about five thousand. And it came to pass on the morrow, that their rulers, and elders, and scribes, And Annas the high priest, and Caiaphas, and John, and Alexander, and as many as were of the kindred of the high priest, were gathered together at Jerusalem.

And when they had set them in the midst, they asked, By what power, or by what name, have ye done this? Then Peter, filled with the Holy Ghost, said unto them, Ye rulers of the people, and elders of Israel, If we this day be examined of the good deed done to the impotent man, by what means he is made whole; Be it known unto you all, and to all the people of Israel, that by the name of Jesus Christ of Nazareth, whom ye crucified, whom God raised from the dead, even by him doth this man stand here before you whole. This is the stone which was set at nought of you builders, which is become the head of the corner. Neither is there salvation in any other: for there is none other name under heaven given among men, whereby we must be saved. Now when they saw the boldness of Peter and John, and perceived that they were unlearned and ignorant men, *they marvelled; and they took knowledge of them, that they had been with Jesus.*

—Acts 4:1–13, emphasis added

Not only did the people "marvel" at them, but the verse goes on to say, "They took knowledge of them, that they had been with Jesus." I love that sentence. There was something different about these men. They had been with Jesus.

We see that the extreme boldness of Peter and John not only astounded the people but it glorified God:

> But Peter and John answered and said unto them, Whether it be right in the sight of God to hearken unto you more than unto God, judge ye. For we cannot but speak the things which we have seen and heard. So when they had further threatened them, they let them go, finding nothing how they might punish them, because of the people: *for all men glorified God for that which was done.*
>
> —ACTS 4:19–21, EMPHASIS ADDED

God is a marvelous wonder-working God. And His Word will always produce the desired result. I believe God's people need to decide they are going to be bold and tell about Jesus, no matter what other people think, no matter what other people say. God's people need to say like Peter and John, "I have to talk about what I have seen, what I've heard, what I've experienced." We need to tell others about Jesus and His wondrous works. We need to speak so boldly and profoundly of Him that people will marvel at us and wonder if we have "been with Jesus." When we speak with boldness and confidence about Jesus, it confirms His Word. It verifies His very character and nature. After demonstrating and proclaiming the marvelous power of God, Peter and John went to give an account to their friends of what had happened to them.

> And being let go, they went to their own company, and reported all that the chief priests and elders had said unto them.
>
> —Acts 4:23

The verse says, "They went to their own company." Dr. Kenneth E. Hagin used to say that everyone needs their own company. What does it mean to need your own company? It means to have your own group—to be a part of a group of people who believe like you believe and who will get united in the things of God. That's why it's so important that God's people belong to a local church. They need a place where they can be fed spiritually in order to grow and thrive, a place where they're under a spiritual covering. You need a company, a place to be in one accord. You need your own group, a place where people will stand with you, pray with you, and seek God with you.

Let's look at what happened when Peter and John came to their own company.

> And when they heard that, they lifted up their voice to God with one accord, and said, Lord, thou art God, which hast made heaven, and earth, and the sea, and all that in them is: Who by the mouth of thy servant David hast said, Why did the heathen rage, and the people imagine vain things? The kings of the earth stood up, and the rulers were gathered together against the Lord, and against his Christ. For of a truth against thy holy child Jesus, whom thou hast anointed, both Herod, and Pontius Pilate, with the Gentiles, and the people of Israel, were gathered together, For to do whatsoever thy hand

> and thy counsel determined before to be done. And now, Lord, *behold their threatenings: and grant unto thy servants, that with all boldness they may speak thy word…*
>
> —ACTS 4:24–29, EMPHASIS ADDED

Peter and John spent very little time talking about the threats that had occurred. They spent most of their time talking about God and how outstanding God is and what they had seen Him do. Peter and John glorified and praised God and exalted His Name. There's a real lesson here about how to respond and pray when things aren't going right. If you and I would do the same thing, we would get far more of our prayers answered. They spoke God's Word with boldness and confidence, and God performed a great healing which resulted in the Lord Jesus being glorified. They proved God to be faithful and true to His Word. They were "proving God." In other words, they were proving that God's Word is true. I'm not talking about "experimenting" with God. I'm not talking about "trying" God. I'm talking about PROVING GOD!

Chapter 3

DON'T BE A WIMP!

To go before Almighty God and present your case requires boldness. You have to be strong and take your stand. Don't be a wimp! No matter if no one else is taking a stand, you have to take your stand. In order to do that, you have to know who your God is. You have to know who you are in Him. You have to be bold before Him like the Syrophoenician woman who came before Jesus seeking help for her daughter. It seemed Jesus was going to deny her request. But she refused to be denied. She took her stand. She boldly spoke up and presented her case to Him saying, "Even the dogs under the master's table get to eat the crumbs." Because of her boldness to speak up and reason with Him, Jesus granted her request and delivered her daughter because of her faith (Mark 7:25–30). Glory to God!

Think about the woman with the issue of blood who came to Jesus to be healed (Matthew 9:20–22). What an example of boldness! This woman's bleeding condition made her "unclean" according to Jewish law. In that culture, a person who was unclean had to avoid contact with other people. If they left their home, they had to shout "unclean" as they walked along. If they failed to abide by the Law, they could be stoned to death. Think about this woman's predicament. She was coming to Jesus to receive her healing. But there was a problem. Jesus was walking with Jairus, the ruler of the synagogue. This man had the authority to have her stoned for being in public, which, according to the law, was a crime. That would be the same as if you had just committed a crime and you walked up to someone who was standing with a policeman. Now you have a problem. You know the one with the policeman will show you mercy and protect you from penalty of the law. You are determined and press on despite the possible consequences. You have to get to the one who will show you mercy, just like this woman had to get to Jesus. This woman knew Jairus could have her stoned, but she didn't care. She was "going for it." She was determined to get to Jesus. She believed He would show her mercy. Her determination resulted in her being rewarded for her faith. And what a reward she received! She was made whole, receiving complete healing and total restoration. Glory to God!

The same is as true for us as it was for those two women. We must be determined to get our healing, or whatever it is we need from God. We do it by the Word of God. We must prove God and His Word! We can't prove anything until we take God at His Word. Believe the Word, then speak the Word, and then the Word will prove itself. Most people want the Word to prove itself first, and then they'll believe it. What they're really saying is, "I'll know I'm healed when my body tells me I'm healed. I'll know I'm prosperous when I've got money in the bank." That doesn't require any faith. It takes a great deal of faith to say you have something when all the evidence is to the contrary. It takes faith to say something totally different than what the medical reports and the doctors say and even different from what your body says or how you feel. But that's exactly what we have to do. We have to believe we have it before we see it. But you can "see it" through faith in God's Word. That's the only way to prove God's Word—through eyes of faith.

We all have problems. Some problems are big problems—mountain-size problems. In Mark 11:23 Jesus tells us how to deal with problems.

> For verily I say unto you, That whosever shall *say* unto this mountain, Be thou removed, and be cast into the sea; and shall not doubt in his heart, but shall believe that those things which he saith shall come to pass; he shall have whatsoever he *saith* (emphasis added).

Jesus says we have to SAY something to the mountain (the obstacle or problem). Jesus tells us to talk to the problem. We aren't supposed to talk *about* the problem; we are to talk *to* the problem and tell it how big our God is! Say to the problem (the mountain), "I don't care how big you are. My God is greater. In the Name of Jesus, be removed and cast into the sea!" Speaking to the problem is the key. Our speaking in faith is what will chip away at that mountain and eventually cause it to crumble. When we speak to the mountain, we are not just speaking as ourselves. We are speaking the truth as righteous, justified children of God endued with power, to whom the nature of God has been imputed. We speak with the authority of God because we are speaking His Word and speaking in His Name.

God has made you a vessel of honor. The Spirit of God lives in you. You have to allow Him to have precedence in your life. You have to be full—saturated—with the Word of God and the Spirit of God so that when you speak to that mountain you know it's not just you but God and His Word speaking. When you speak by the power and Spirit of God you don't just ask the mountain to move. You tell it to go in Jesus' Name. Speak to that problem, that situation, and believe it will bow to the Word of God.

Believing. That is a key to operating in the power and

authority God has given to us. Paul the Apostle tells the Ephesians about a prayer he prayed regularly:

> That the God of our Lord Jesus Christ, the Father of glory, may give unto you the spirit of wisdom and revelation in the knowledge of him: The eyes of your understanding being enlightened; that ye may know what is the hope of his calling, and what the riches of the glory of his inheritance in the saints, And what is the exceeding greatness of his *power to us-ward who believe*, according to the working of his mighty power…
>
> —Ephesians 1:17–19, emphasis added

Notice the phrase "And what is the exceeding greatness of his power *to us who believe*." God's power being released to you has nothing to do with Him. It has to do with you and your believing Him and His Word. Have you ever pondered that? Think about it for a moment. Those who believe are the ones who receive. If we truly believe, then we will receive His power to operate in and through us. We have to believe in Him, believe that He cannot lie, believe that His Word is true, believe that His Word is working mightily in us, believe that His Word will bring a change in our circumstances. Those who believe are the ones who receive. One of the definitions of the word *receive* in the Greek language is "to take." We TAKE from God by faith that which He has already provided. For example, He has already provided our healing. Our part is to take it by faith.

The Bible clearly teaches us how to deal with situations, circumstances, and problems that arise in our lives. James 5:13–16 says:

> Is any among you afflicted? let him pray. Is any merry? let him sing psalms. Is any sick among you? let him call for the elders of the church; and let them pray over him, anointing him with oil in the name of the Lord: And the prayer of faith shall save the sick, and the Lord shall raise him up; and if he have committed sins, they shall be forgiven him. Confess your [trespasses] to one another, and pray for one another, that you may be healed. The [effective] fervent prayer of a righteous man avails much.

What is James saying here? Is there anyone among you afflicted, suffering, in trials or difficulties? Well then, let him pray. So many people will go to the pastor and say, "Pray for me, preacher. I'm having a difficult time, pray for me. Things are bad. Pray for me. I'm going through trials. Pray for me." The Bible says pray for yourself. If you are afflicted, troubled, bothered, having problems, then pray! Present your case to God and expect Him to intervene. Then he asks, "Is any merry? Let him sing psalms." When we're merry, we should be singing and praising God. Then he asks, "Is any sick among you? Let him call for the elders of the church; and let them pray over him, anointing him with oil in the name of the Lord. And the prayer of faith shall save the sick, and the Lord shall raise him up." Is any among you sick? They should call for the elders of the church, and they are to pray over him, anointing him with oil in the Name of the Lord. The Lord will heal that one and raise him up. "*The effectual fervent prayer of a righteous man availeth much*" (verse 16). *Availeth* means "accomplishes much." The power of prayer that is offered in faith can change problems into victories. In truth, the victory is already present, but the problem blocks it from view. Prayer simply reveals the victory.

James goes on to speak about Elijah. "[Elijah] was a man subject to like passions as we are, and he prayed earnestly that it might not rain: and it rained not on the earth by the space of three years and six months. And he prayed again, and the heaven gave rain…(James 5:17–18). Elijah was a righteous man of God. When presented with a problem, he prayed earnestly and his prayers accomplished what he was seeking from God. Once Elijah received the Word of the Lord, he boldly acted on it. That's what we're supposed to do—receive the Word of God, act boldly on the Word of God, and prove the Word of God!

The Bible admonishes us in Romans 12:2, "Be not conformed to this world; but be ye transformed by the renewing of your mind, that ye may prove what is that good, and acceptable, and perfect, will of God." You may have thought at times, "If I only knew God's will." The Bible tells us we can know and prove God's will. How? By having our minds renewed by the Word of God. According to 2 Timothy 3:16, "All scripture is given by inspiration of God, and is profitable for doctrine, for reproof, for correction, for instruction." All scripture is profitable or beneficial for us. But you will have to read, study, and meditate on the Word to renew your mind, think differently, and look at the situation differently. Then present your case to God, bring His Word boldly before Him and expect Him to work on your behalf!

Chapter 4
HE SAVES TO THE UTTERMOST

YOU MAY ASK, "Does God's redemptive work really take care of *every* area of my life?" Did Jesus really take care of every need at the cross of Calvary? Do you believe that God took care of your spirit through the forgiveness of sins? Most Christians believe that. So, if He took care of the spirit, wouldn't He also take care of the soul (mind, will, and emotions)? He has made it so you can control your emotions, your attitudes, and your thinking. Romans 12:2 tells us how: Be transformed by the renewing of your mind through the Word of God. James 1:21 says that the engrafted Word of God can save your soul. But what about the body? Did God make provision for our bodies? The Bible says Jesus went about doing three things: teaching, preaching, and HEALING. Hebrews tells us *Jesus is the same yesterday, today, and forever* (Hebrews 13:8). Therefore healing is for today. Yet most churches today leave out one third of the gospel since they do not teach healing.

The Bible says Jesus came to destroy the works of the devil (1 John 3:8). The works of the devil include sickness and disease. Jesus came to destroy disease, and He did just that! He went about healing all that were sick. The only time Jesus could not heal was in His own hometown, where the people's unbelief stopped Him. We have to dare to believe and stand firm on God's Word. Even though the Bible says something, it doesn't make it real for us until we prove it.

We have to believe that God will perform His Word totally and completely. Hebrews 7:25 says, "Wherefore he is able also to save them to the uttermost that come unto God by him, seeing he ever liveth to make intercession for them." God is able to "save to the uttermost" those who draw near to Him. How do you draw near to Him? Through Jesus. God is able to save you to the uttermost because Jesus the Great Intercessor is interceding for you and me. He is in Heaven right now interceding for you before the throne of God. What does the word *uttermost* mean? It means fully, completely, extreme, highest degree. The word *save* comes from the Greek word *sozo,* which means "save, heal, deliver, preserve." God is able to save to the uttermost. He is able to save fully, completely, to the extreme, highest degree. God does not partially save. He does not partially heal. He does not partially deliver. Whatever God does, He does it to the uttermost! He goes all the way with you. There is nothing beyond His ability because He saves to the uttermost. The issue is whether or not we can believe what He says. That's what it all comes down to. Do we believe God and His Word? The word "believe" carries the meaning of "trust." Do we trust God to be true to His Word?

Sometimes when I'm sharing the wonderful Word, or promises, of God, people will say, "You're giving false hope." Are you kidding? How can I be giving "false hope" when I'm quoting the Word of God? His Word is pure truth! There is nothing false about it. Should I tell people there is no hope when the Bible is filled with hope? The Bible is filled with the love, hope, grace, and mercy of God!

God is not against us. God is on our side. He expects us to trust Him. We have to ask ourselves, "Can I trust God?" That's a very important question. And even if our answer is yes, we have to ask ourselves, "Can I trust God with whatever comes my way?" It's easy to answer yes but not actually believe it in our hearts. We absolutely have to make a decision to trust God no matter what the situation or how difficult it appears to be. God is in the creating business. He is in the miracle business. He is in the restoration business. He can create things. He can make miracles happen. He can restore anything that needs to be restored.

God is not disturbed by dead things. He is not upset over dead marriages, dead finances, not even dead body parts. He can restore a dead marriage and bring it to life again. God can work in the midst of financial disaster and miraculously provide finances. He can create new organs for someone willing to accept and take them by faith. The Word of God is alive and full of power. He wants us to speak His living Word and watch dead things come back to life! It's a matter of trusting God. It requires stepping out in faith. Sometimes we're not comfortable doing that. But remember . . . to be called an overcomer means I have overcome something. If I'm a conqueror, it means I have conquered something. If I'm the "head and not the tail," then I have risen above situations and circumstances.

Faith requires action on our part. We have to do something and then trust God to do His part. So often people don't want to take a leap without God catching them first. But He can't catch you until you jump! It's a leap of faith! We make that leap based on God's Word.

What you are now experiencing of God has to do with how you have sought Him, how you have trusted Him, whether or not you have believed Him, and whether or not you have been willing to step out on the things of God. There comes a time when we have to make decisions. I've seen people come right to the point of a decision and stop. They just won't do it. They won't press in, won't make the necessary effort. Why not make a decision to trust God to the uttermost and go all the way with Him? I'll tell you why people won't go all the way. Fear. Fear is the opposite of faith. Fear says, "This isn't going to work. This doesn't make sense. I can't possibly do that." When I faced the decision to trust God and become a minister, people would say to me, "If you become a preacher, you'll perish. You'll starve to death." They were so wrong. They were in fear. If I had listened to them and allowed fear to stop me from obeying the call of God on my life, I would not be here today being used of God. And I would have missed out on seeing God do the miraculous and spectacular over the years.

In Mark 9:23 a man comes to Jesus seeking help for his son who was tormented by an evil spirit. "Jesus said unto him, if thou canst believe, *all things are possible* to him that believeth" (emphasis added). Luke 1:37 says, "For with God *nothing is ever impossible* and no word from God shall be without power or impossible of fulfillment" (AMP, emphasis added). Remember, *nothing* is impossible with God. That's what the Word says—nothing. He says we are to come to Him and ask. Can I ask only for certain things and not others? Does that mean I can only ask for salvation and not for healing? Does it mean I can ask for salvation and not for deliverance? Does it mean I can't ask for prosperity? Does it mean I can't ask for creative miracles? Does it mean that I'm limited in what I can ask? The Bible teaches that we "have not because we *ask not*" (James 4:3, emphasis added)." We have a right to go to God and ask for what we need or desire of Him, but we should have the right motive in our asking. It would be like going to someone and asking, "Why do you want to be healed?" and then they answer, "So I can play a game of tennis." Someone else might answer, "So I can go jogging again." Someone else might say, "So I can have fun." No. Wrong answer! The reason we should want to be healed should be the same reason we want to be saved—so we can serve the living God, make a difference in this world, and cause someone to see that God is still alive and moving in this earth. We should want to be delivered so others can see that God is faithful and will do what He said He would do.

Your testimony will encourage others who are going through similar circumstances. We know if He did it for one, He will do it for another because He is no respecter of persons (Acts 10:34). But we have to prove Him. We have to prove that what He has said is true. As a matter of fact, God basically says for us to prove whether His Word is right or wrong. God is saying to us, "Come on. Let's talk. Let's talk about My Word."

Psalm 103:1–2 says, "Bless the Lord, O my soul." Your soul is your mind, will, and emotions. "Bless the Lord, O my soul" is the same thing as saying "Bless the Lord, O my thinking processes." Bless the Lord, thinking processes! You may say, "Well, you don't understand my situation. You don't know how bad things are at my house, and it never changes." The reason things never change for you isn't because God won't do something about your situation. It's because you're not convinced that He will, and you won't give God room to move. We have to say to ourselves, "Bless the Lord, O my thinking processes. Bless the Lord, O my mind, bless the Lord. Mind…don't you forget His benefits. Mind, straighten up. Don't you forget what He has done."

Perhaps your situation is that you need healing. Maybe you even need a new body part, like an arm or foot or kidney or liver. Listen, God making you a new creation is far more miraculous than His creating a new body part! When you were saved (born again), He made you "brand spanking new" inside, acceptable to God, so new, so clean, so holy that God Himself would live inside you. This was a far greater work than healing or even creating a body part. But the Word says He *has* made you new and clean and holy. You *are* a new creation in Christ Jesus (2 Cor. 5:17, emphasis added). So, what is there to a simple repair job for your body? That's what healing is, a repair job. God said, "I will restore health unto thee, and I will heal thee of thy wounds" (Jeremiah 30:17).

God says to us, "Come, let's talk. Come, present your case. Come, let's reason together." Don't just throw out some statement and wonder what's going to happen. The Bible tells us what is going to happen. You will get exactly what God's Word says you will get. So, when you speak God's Word, expect to get what the Word says, with no wavering or doubting. Keep your eyes on a definite result, an expected outcome. The Bible gives definite results, not maybe's. If you need healing, expect to be healed. God did not say, "I will heal you—*maybe*." He didn't say, "By My stripes, *possibly* you are healed." He has said that by His stripes you ARE healed (Isaiah 53:5). He didn't say, "I sent My Word and *thought about* healing you." He said very clearly, "I sent My Word and healed you" (Psalm 107:20).

If God said "one plus one equals two," you wouldn't question that. You wouldn't think that was strange. Why? Because you understand mathematics. The trouble is that we tend to believe more in mathematics than we do in prayer and the Word. The Bible gives us definite results, just as definite as the laws of mathematics. If God says, "By My stripes you are healed," why would we be surprised when we're healed? Our faith needs to be in God's Word. His Word is a sure word. Stay focused. Stay tuned in to His Word. Once you have asked God for something based on His Word, don't change what you're expecting. Don't give in to doubts. Protect your faith. Be immovable in every circumstance. Refuse to be denied!

When confronted by the enemy, Jesus simply said, "It is written" and then quoted the Word of God (Matthew 4:1–11). When we are confronted by the enemy with symptoms or difficulties, we absolutely MUST quote the Word of God. We must stand firm on what is written just like Jesus did. The Word is our weapon!

Chapter 5
SAY AMEN!

SECOND CORINTHIANS 1:20 says, "For all the promises of God in him are yea, and in him Amen, unto the glory of God by us." It doesn't say the promises are sometimes yes and sometimes no. They are "yes" and they are "amen." Amen means "so be it." Amen is in agreement with "yes." We must agree with what God says. Every promise of God has already been fulfilled. As far as He's concerned, all of them are "yes." If God says He is our healer, then we should expect healing to take place. If God is our deliverer, then we should expect deliverance to take place. If God is our caretaker, then we should expect Him to take care of us. If He's our provider, then we should expect God to provide for us. Why? Because all of God's promises are "yes" and "amen." Everything God has promised has a "yes" attached to it!

We're not trying to get God to do something. It's already been done! God has completed all of His work. He's resting. And He wants us to rest with Him because He has done everything He needs to do about your situation. It's a done deal! You can rest with God. Jesus said that we are to be anxious for nothing (Philippians 4:6). And the Bible tells us "In everything give thanks" (1 Thessalonians 5:18). And it tells us to praise Him. Why praise Him? Because of His promises. Your part is to say, "Amen." Saying "Amen" means you are in agreement with what He has said. God says, "I'll never leave you nor forsake you." Well, you say, "Amen." God says, "Greater is He who is in you than he who is in the world." You say, "Amen."

God says, "He who calls you is faithful who will also do it." You say, "Amen." Your answer is "Amen!"

In Matthew 18:19, Jesus speaks of the prayer of agreement. "Again I say unto you, that *if two of you shall agree on earth* as touching any thing that they shall ask, it shall be done for them of my Father which is in heaven" (emphasis added). He is talking about two or more people coming into agreement with each other based on their knowledge of God's will. God's Word and His will are one and the same. The prayer of agreement is a powerful type of prayer. When you speak or pray the Word of God, you are in agreement with God. You are agreeing with what He has said. You need to get someone to stand in agreement with you, agreeing with what God's Word says.

I know it seems that God sometimes waits until the last minute to fulfill His promise. He has a way of showing up at 11:59, the last moment before the midnight hour. Most people give up too soon, not willing to WAIT and trust that God will show up. You have to stand with God until you receive what you have asked for in faith. You stand until it has manifested. Don't move off of it. Don't change your confession. Don't say, "Well, I guess this is not working." You've got to persevere! Remember, when we speak, we are actually prophesying. With our mouths, we can prophesy good or bad. If you speak, "Well, I guess it's not working," you just prophesied failure. You've just come into agreement with the devil instead of God. That verse that says "if two of you agree" is speaking of two *believers* agreeing. That's why if you need healing, it's bad to be involved in a church that doesn't teach healing or even believe in healing. If you are in a church like that, then you need to find someone who believes in healing to stand with you in agreement with the Word of God for your healing. It's easy to find folks who will *say* they agree with you. But if they have no knowledge of the Word, particularly about healing, they're just doing the "religious" thing and saying they agree with you. Also, people will tend to speak negative things, things that don't line up with the Word. Do you know what you do with those people? You run from them! We're talking life-and-death issues here!

You've got to have people standing with you who are strong in the Word of God. Jesus was speaking that verse to believers. He was saying that when two believer*s* agree, they shall have anything they ask. Find a believer to agree with you—a believer in Jesus, a believer in the full gospel which includes healing. Find yourself someone who will agree with you based on what God has said about healing. Find yourself "four crazy friends" like the paralyzed man had (Mark 2:3). Have them stand in faith with you and prophesy the Word of the Lord—over you, for you, and with you.

The Bible says that Heaven and earth shall pass away, but His Word will not pass away (Matthew 24:35). Jesus said in John 15:7 that if we abide in Him and His words abide in us, we can ask what we will and it will be done for us. Having His words abide in us means they remain and continue to live in us. The Word says that all things are possible with God (Matthew 19:26). There's nothing impossible when we are "with" God. Being "with" God means we are likeminded with Him, we are aligned with Him, we are in agreement with Him. We just have to agree with Him and His Word.

Mark 11:24 says, "Therefore I say unto you, What things soever ye desire, when ye pray, believe that ye receive them, and ye shall have them." When you pray, believe that you receive. That's a prayer of faith. What is a prayer of faith? It's simply agreeing with God based on His Word. Whatever your request is, you've settled it in your heart and believe you receive it. You have to be diligent and persistent. When something opposite of what you're believing for happens, you say, "No! That's not what I agreed for. I agreed for what God's Word says." You have to stand firm on what you believe, stay on it, and refuse to move off of it.

I recall at one of our meetings we were expecting to gain a certain number of new partners. We agreed and then we asked the Lord for that number. After the meeting when almost everyone had left, my staff reported to me the number of those who had signed up as new partners. They were rejoicing over the number of new partners, and talking about the generous amounts the new partners were giving. But we were one short of the number we had agreed for. I looked at them and said, "We did not ask God for a certain amount that they would give. We asked Him for a certain number of new partners. And we're one short. Go and check again." I received a call later, and they reported that another partner had come in and we got the exact number we were expecting.

I've seen the prayer of agreement work over and over again. You have to be willing to say, "Count one more time. We agreed on this number. Count again. It's impossible for it not to be there." But what happens so often is we settle for less than what we were expecting. We give up. We must learn to stand firm. Never give up! Only believe and keep on believing!

Perhaps you don't think you are worthy of receiving what God has promised. You may be saying, "Oh, but I've done all kinds of things since I met Jesus. I have sinned in so many ways. I have fallen short of the glory of God. I have missed it so many times." Well, your heavenly Father has made a provision for dealing with our sin problems:

> If we confess our sins, he is faithful and just to forgive us our sins, and to cleanse us from all unrighteousness.
>
> —1 JOHN 1:9

When we repent, He cleanses us from every sin and all unrighteousness. We simply confess our sins to Him and repent and we know that He forgives us instantly. In fact, in His mind it's like it never happened. He does not want us wallowing around in a pit of guilt and condemnation. He wants us to believe His Word, then rush quickly to His throne, confess our sins, repent, then accept the forgiveness He has provided for us. In Isaiah 43:25, He says "I, even I, am he that blotteth out thy transgressions for mine own sake, and will not remember thy sins." Having your transgressions blotted out is being justified through the Blood of Jesus. When Jesus came, He made a way for us to be forgiven of all our sins in the sight of God. You don't have to beg God for forgiveness. Believers are not beggars. Simply go to Him, ask for forgiveness, and thank Him for forgiving and cleansing you. You can depend on Him to do that because He said He would.

Remember, "repentance" means a turning away, a changing of your direction. If we've been going in the wrong direction, the way of sin, the Lord expects us to turn around and change direction. Once you've repented, it's done. Don't walk in guilt and condemnation over that thing. Your sins have been forgiven. The Bible says He has no record of them. It's as if they have been cast into a sea of forgetfulness. You don't ever have to worry about standing in front of the throne of God and facing one of your sins—not if you've asked for forgiveness. Glory to God! It's gone! Some people may say something like, "Well, I know why this has happened to you...because you did thus and so." Well, you may have done thus and so, but if you have asked God to forgive you, that sin is gone. You've turned the page and you're now starting on a new page! The new page does not start off with hours of repenting constantly, over and over. No, it begins with shouting—shouting praise and thanksgiving to God because He has said, "For I will be merciful to their unrighteousness, and their sins and their iniquities will I remember no more" (Hebrews 8:12).

There are arrogant, religious people that want to tell you, "Well now...we can't demand things of God." I'm not demanding anything of God, I'm demanding that the devil turn loose what God says belongs to me! I'm commanding the devil to get out of my way in the Name of Jesus. I'm not commanding God to do anything. I am simply accepting what He's already done for me. I am simply coming before God and asking for what is rightfully mine based on what He has already provided for me.

Consider 1 John 5:14–15: "And this is the confidence that we have in him, that, if we ask any thing according to his will, he heareth us: And if we know that he hear us, whatsoever we ask, we know that we have the petitions that we desired of him." Well, there's the problem. Many people don't know His will. They don't know His will because they have not read His Word. Since they don't know His will, they don't know what they can ask of Him. God said, "My people perish for lack of knowledge" (Hosea 4:6). That's why it is imperative that we know and understand God's Word. We think, "Well, if I can just get Him to hear me..." How do you get God to hear you? You ask according to His will. You ask according to His Word. For instance, what if you need healing? How can you know the will of God concerning healing? You go to the Bible and find out what God says about healing. The Bible says in Psalm 107:20, "I sent my Word and healed them." Isaiah 53:5 says, "With His stripes, we are healed," and in 1 Peter 2:24, "By whose stripes ye were healed." According to the Bible, healing is His will. The leper said to Jesus in Matthew 8:2, "Lord, if thou wilt, thou canst make me clean." You may be saying, "God, I know You *can*, but *will* You?" What did Jesus say to the leper? He said, *I* WILL. He didn't say, "I'll think about it" or "Come back tomorrow and maybe I will heal you." No! Jesus said, "I will." There was never a time in the Bible when Jesus said no to someone who came to Him for healing. Never. The only time He didn't heal was in His hometown because they would not believe in Him (Matthew 13:58). But everyone who came to Him asking and believing received their healing. Jesus is our sin-bearer. And He is our sickness-bearer. That's what His Word says. Here are just a few of the scriptures which speak of Him as our sin-bearer and sickness-bearer:

> So Christ was once offered to bear the sins of many…
>
> —HEBREWS 9:28

> Surely he hath borne our griefs [sicknesses], and carried our sorrows [pains]…But he was wounded for our transgressions, he was bruised for our iniquities: the chastisement for our peace was upon him; and with his stripes we are healed.
>
> —ISAIAH 53:4–5

> That it might be fulfilled which was spoken by [Isaiah] the prophet, saying, Himself took our infirmities, and bare our sicknesses.
>
> —Matthew 8:17

> Who his own self bare our sins in his own body on the tree, that we, being dead to sins, should live unto righteousness: by whose stripes ye were healed.
>
> —1 Peter 2:24

Let's look again at 1 John 5:14–15. It says, "This is the *confidence* that we have in him, that, if we ask any thing according to his will, he heareth us: And if we know that he hear us, whatsoever we ask, we know that we have the petitions that we desired of him" (emphasis added). It says we have confidence. It doesn't say "we hope." It says "This is the confidence we have." We KNOW. We KNOW that we receive. We know we have the petitions, the requests, the things we have asked of Him. We know we receive when we ask according to His Word. Whatever it is that you need or desire of God, find the scriptures that show God's will in that area. Keep prophesying. Keep believing that you will have what God says you can have! That is a key that can transform your entire life!

Chapter 6
HE BRINGS DEAD THINGS TO LIFE!

God told Abraham that he and Sarah would have a son. There was just one problem. Abraham was an old man with an old wife. They were far beyond life-bearing years. In essence, they were more dead than alive. But God is a life-giver. The Bible says that God brings dead things to life, and He calls those things that be not as though they were (Romans 4:17).

All of us have "dead things" in our lives. It may be a problem with your health, or your marriage may seem like it's dead, or your finances or job may seem to be dead. We have to speak life into "dead things!" God says, "Call those things that be not as though they were." In other words, call it the way you want it to be based on God's Word. Quit calling it the way you see it in the natural realm. Call those "dead things" back to life again. Call them to be what you want, not just what you have.

Abraham was nearly 100 years old, yet he made up his mind to believe God. I believe his thoughts might have gone something like this: "I better not look at this body, and I sure better not look at Sarah's body!" He made up his mind real fast. When he received the promise of God that he would have a son, I believe he thought to himself, "I'm going to look one way and one way only—Godward. I'm going to look at God and keep looking at God. I'm going to keep my eyes on God. I'm going to abide in God. I've heard what God said, and I'm simply going to believe it. I'm not looking at Sarah's old dead body. If I glance at Sarah, it'll cause me to come out of faith. If I look in the mirror, it'll cause me to come out of faith. I'm going to keep looking at God, and I'm going to quote His promise morning, noon, and night. I have blinders on. I'm looking at God and Him only. I'm going to remind myself continually of what He said. I know that God cannot lie. This is what He said, and if He said it, He will do it. I'll just keep my eyes on God and what He said, and I will not waver. We will produce a son!"

Of course, Abraham and Sarah had to work with God. They had to do their part. You have to do your part. Real faith always has corresponding action. If you can't walk but God says you can walk, you've got to try to walk. If you can't talk, but He says you can talk, you've got to try to talk. That's what Abraham did. He believed God more than he believed his own body, Sarah's body, or their circumstances. The Bible says Abraham was "fully persuaded" that what God had promised, He was able to perform (Romans 4:21). The more we focus on what God said, the more things will begin to happen. If God has spoken it, you can be fully persuaded that He will bring it to pass. This is where people miss it so often. They say, "I tried, and it didn't work." If God said it, you can bank on it! You have to find the promise of God and then speak (prophesy) that Word in faith and prove His Word is true and that it will produce the promise. He didn't say it would always happen the first time you speak His Word. God wants you to stand on His Word and not waver. He wants you to have Abraham-like faith and be fully persuaded! How can we be fully persuaded, unwavering, and strong in faith? We can do the same thing Abraham did. In verse 20, it says "He staggered not at the promises of God through unbelief but was strong in faith, GIVING

GLORY TO GOD." Did you get that? The Bible calls "giving glory to God" strong faith! It's a decision to be in agreement with God and His Word. It's a decision to believe God and give Him glory no matter what circumstances may look like. Forget all the contradictions that come from common sense, worldly thinking, or natural circumstances and be fully persuaded that God can and will perform His Word in your life. Abraham staggered not. He was not moved by what He saw or felt in the natural realm. He was rooted and grounded in the Word of God. He was strong in faith, giving glory to God! He gave glory to God because He knew He would see the fulfillment of God's promise. Every time someone said, "Abraham, you're too old to have a son," Abraham said, "Well…glory to God!" When people said Sarah couldn't have a baby, Abraham said, "Well…glory to God!" That strong faith produced the child God had promised. When the doctors say you can't be healed, say, "Well…glory to God!" When they say your marriage can't survive, say, "Well…glory to God!" When everything looks like it is contrary to the Word of God, well…glory to God! Giving glory to God…that's strong faith!

Calling things the way you want them to be rather than just the way they appear to be is prophesying. You can prophesy. You can speak in the Name of the Lord and "life" something with the Word of God. You can speak what you want or need into being. Prophesying is speaking the mind and the counsel of God. How do we speak the mind and counsel of God? We speak His Word! You can prophesy to a "mountain" in your way (Mark 11:23). You can prophesy with assurance to the "mountains"—dead things, obstacles, or problems—in your life and expect them to be removed, brought to life, or changed.

In John , chapter 11, we find the account of Lazarus. He

and his sisters, Mary and Martha, lived in Bethany and were friends of Jesus. Lazarus had become sick and later died. His sisters had sent word to Jesus that Lazarus was very ill and to come quickly; however, Jesus stayed two days longer in Jerusalem. When He arrived in Bethany, Martha ran out to meet Him and said, "Lord, if you had been here, he would not have died." Jesus told her, "I am the resurrection and the life. He who believes in Me will live and those who believe in Me will never die." He asked her if she believed that. She said, "Yes, I believe You are the Son of God." Then Mary came out to Jesus and said the same thing, "Lord, if you had been here, my brother would not have died." Is that what you've been saying? "Lord, if You had been here this would not have happened." We should never say that to God. He is always with us. He has promised that He is our ever present help. But what you *can* say to yourself is "I need to prophesy! I need to speak and declare the Word of the Lord over this situation." Then do not stop prophesying the Word until you see that "dead thing" come back to life, until you see that situation turn around, until you see it change!

Jesus told Mary, "Did I not say to you that if you believe you will see the glory of God?" Mary and Martha and everyone else who was there were about to see the glory of God. Jesus went to where Lazarus was buried. Then He made an interesting statement (verse 41). He said, "Father, I thank You that You have heard Me." Wait a minute, He hadn't said anything yet. He hadn't prayed yet. But He said, "Father, I thank You that You have heard Me." What did Jesus mean by that? If we look at verse 4 we see that He had previously said, "This sickness is not unto death, but for the glory of God, that the Son of God may be glorified through it." In verse 11, He said, "Our friend Lazarus sleeps [is dead], but I go that I may wake him up." Jesus had prophesied! He had prophesied what the outcome would be. He knew He would raise Lazarus up! Then He acted in accordance with what He had prophesied. He spoke to Lazarus. He said, "Lazarus, come forth." And he that was dead came forth, from death to life. He rose up from the dead and walked out of that tomb! We have to speak to the "dead things" in our lives (health, marriage, etc.) and call them forth from death to life.

There were two phases in this event. The first was when Jesus said, "Lazarus come forth." The second was when Jesus said, "Loose him and let him go." In other words, "Get those grave clothes off of him." What good was it for him to come out of the grave and have him walking around like a mummy? So Lazarus came out and everyone was running around saying, "You ought to come see Lazarus!" Some might have said, "Well, I can't see him, he's all wrapped up." Someone had to get him unwrapped, let him go free. There are people in the church who have "come back to life." They've been born again. But no one will unwrap them, no one will help them get the grave clothes off. No one will help them walk in this new life and liberty. No one will disciple them. Someone has to take the "grave clothes" off of them, help them shake off the old life of sin and death and be set free. They need to be taught and stabilized in the Word of God. They have to be taught the truth so they can get free and stay free.

I recently read an article written by a pastor. He said, "I see so many congregations drawing 'corpses' [those dead in sin] into their churches with a nice basketball league, a good daycare, and a fancy building. They do an excellent job at bringing people in, but once they bring them in, they're afraid of offending them with the Word of God." If all they ever hear are funny stories during sermons, what good does it do them? Preachers have watered down the Word so that the Ten Commandments have become the "Ten Suggestions." The threat of eternal hell is never mentioned. The promise of forgiveness is never laid out. They are never brought out of death into eternal life. They are never set free from the grave clothes of sin. They are still wrapped in the stench of sin. It would be like having a dead corpse with nice clothes on it. It still stinks—just like Martha said about Lazarus as he lay in the tomb: "He stinketh." Jesus spoke the Word and brought him to life. But then Jesus completed the work and said, "Take off those grave clothes, unwrap him. Set him free to be what I've called him to be."

So, what are you to do with the "dead things" that need to be brought to life? Find scriptures that apply to your situation and begin to prophesy. If you're not familiar with the Word, find verses that deal with your situation. Once you have located the scriptures, then prophesy to that situation. For instance, if you need healing, you might say, "Lord, Your Word says You've given me abundant life. Your Word is life and health to all my flesh. I receive life through Your Word, and it brings life and healing to every part of my body. I prophesy it." Speak it forth. When you do that, you're releasing healing and health. For example, if someone is diabetic, they could prophesy, "Jesus took my sickness and bore my pain. Therefore, I refuse to allow sickness to dominate my body. The life of God flows through me bringing healing to every fiber of my being. My pancreas secretes the proper amount of insulin for life and health. My blood sugar levels are normal. I prophesy it." You can prophesy, "No evil will befall me, neither shall any plague come near my dwelling, for You have given Your angels charge over me. They keep me in all my ways." You can say, "In my pathway is life, healing, and health. I prophesy it." You can prophesy based on the Word. For instance, "Jesus bore the curse for me, therefore I forbid growths and tumors to inhabit my body. The life of God within me dissolves growths and tumors, and my strength and health are restored. Your Word is manifested in my body causing growths to disappear." Another example: "Arthritis is a thing of the past. Based on Proverbs 3:8, I declare that my bones and joints function properly in the Name of Jesus with no pain. I prophesy it." Prophesy. Simply agree with the Word of God and speak it out loud.

Chapter 7
DEAD BONES RATTLING

THE PROPHET EZEKIEL knew what to do when faced with a "dead situation." He prophesied life into it!

> The hand of the LORD was upon me, and carried me out in the spirit of the LORD, and set me down in the midst of the valley which was full of bones, And caused me to pass by them round about: and, behold, there were very many in the open valley; and, lo, they were very dry. And he said unto me, Son of man, can these bones live? And I answered, O Lord GOD, thou knowest. Again he said unto me, *Prophesy* upon these bones, and say unto them, O ye dry bones, hear the word of the LORD. Thus saith the Lord GOD unto these bones; Behold, I will cause breath to enter into you, and ye shall live: And I will lay sinews upon you, and will bring up flesh upon you, and cover you with skin, and put breath in you, and ye shall live; and ye shall know that I am the LORD. So I *prophesied* as I was commanded: and as I prophesied, there was a noise, and behold a shaking, and the bones came together, bone to his bone. And when I beheld, lo, the sinews and the flesh came up upon them, and the skin covered them above: but there was no breath in them. Then said he unto me, *Prophesy* unto the wind, *prophesy*, son of man, and say to the wind, Thus saith the Lord GOD; Come from the four winds, O breath, and breathe upon

> these slain, that they may live. So *I prophesied* as he commanded me, and the breath came into them, and they lived, and stood up upon their feet, an exceeding great army.
>
> —EZEKIEL 37:1–10, EMPHASIS ADDED

By faith Ezekiel spoke to those dead, dry bones. Just like him, we are to prophesy. God tells us to speak His counsel, to speak His Word over the "dry bones" of our lives. Perhaps you are thinking, "But Ezekiel was a priest and a prophet. He was called to prophesy." Revelation 1:6 says we have been made kings and priests unto God. Once you are born again, washed in the Blood of the Lamb, you belong to God. You are justified, made righteous and indwelt by the Holy Spirit. The enemy does not want you to know who you are in Christ. He wants you to think you are a nobody. Why does he tell that lie? Because if we think we're an unworthy nobody, we won't have the faith and confidence to speak forth the Word of the Lord. You have to know who you are and know that you are in right standing with God. You are a king and a priest unto the Lord. You are more than a conqueror in this life! You are an overcomer! It's not based on what you feel. It's certainly not based on your past. God is greater than all of it! God absolutely *will* forgive you. In fact, He has already done it. Your sins can be eradicated, done away with, in the twinkling of an eye. God is just waiting for someone that knows who they are in Him to be bold and rise to the occasion. He's waiting for someone that knows they are a king and a priest unto Him to step up and take their rightful place and prophesy! He's waiting on you and me! Prophesy and prove that the Word of the Lord is true and powerful enough to change your situation!

Why is it that so many people do not step into their

rightful place and prophesy? One problem is that people have been taught to be quiet. Some churches don't allow people to say "amen," much less anything else. Many of us have been taught to be quiet in church. We think being quiet is being holy. Well, then...we ought to have our church service in a cemetery! It's real quiet in a cemetery! The church should be a noisy place. We should be praising and worshipping God. We should be speaking forth the counsel of God. We must know who we are and act like it. If we don't, we'll become like dry bones. We cannot live contrary to the Word and expect the things of God to be manifested in our lives. If God says "speak," then speak. Don't yield and bow to evil forces that want to keep the Church silent.

As I was reading this passage, I kept wondering, "What is it about Ezekiel? Why could he speak to dry bones and see them come to life?" I researched and discovered that according to the sages and rabbis of old it was because he was a righteous man. Righteousness is the key to resurrection life. Everyone who is born again has been made righteous by the Blood of Jesus. Prophesy by the voice of the Spirit of God which dwells in you. Prophesy, just like when Ezekiel spoke. Sinews, flesh, skin, and bones will respond to the Spirit of God. You can speak with power and authority to your body and expect it to respond to the Word and the Spirit of God. You can also speak to other areas of your life and expect the same results. Take charge of your life! Take charge over your marriage, your children, your home, your business, your finances, your body. Speak to those dead things in the Name of Jesus and command them to come to life! For instance, call your marriage back to life. Call your business "prosperous" and expect it to be successful and to flourish. Prophesy that you will walk in the prosperity of the

Lord. "I will have a job!" "I will have money in the bank!" "I will work in might and power for the glory of God!" Prophesy. "I will be who God has called me to be!" Stand on the Word of God and prophesy that your children will be saved and will serve the Lord. "I call my children into the Kingdom of God. I prophesy over them in the Name of the Lord that they will be servants of the Living God!" If you're wanting to conceive a child, prophesy a baby into your womb. Say, "Psalm 127:3 says that children are a heritage of the Lord. Barrenness is a part of the curse and Jesus has redeemed me from the curse. Therefore, I will be fruitful and multiply and produce children." Prove the Word of the Lord. Prove that it IS true. The key to life is to believe what God has said. Those who believe will receive. Speak the Word of God boldly!

Ezekiel prophesied the Word of the Lord to those dry bones. Keep in mind that it's not just YOUR word that makes dead things come to life again. It's your speaking the Word of the Lord. You may not know or understand how God is going to do it, but you can be sure you will get the end result God has spoken.

Take note, there were two phases Ezekiel had to complete before the dead, dry bones became an exceedingly great army. In verse 8: "And when I beheld, lo, the sinews and the flesh came up upon them, and the skin covered them above," we see that flesh came back on those dead, dry bones. But there was still a problem, as the verse shows us: "But there was no breath in them." Sometimes it's easy to get people to start something. They will do the first part, go about half way, and then stop. They'll hear the bones rattling and get all excited. And then they'll see the sinews, flesh, and skin come upon dead, dry bones. And they'll get excited and run and tell someone about it. "You won't believe what happened! You have to come and see! Bones got up from here and from there! And one came from this place and another came from that place! They were flying from here and from there! They all connected themselves together! You never heard such rattling! Not only did the bones come together, but then flesh and sinews and skin came upon them! Oh, I wish you could have been there to see what God just did!"

It's great that they are all excited, but they're just settling, stopping halfway. So what are they left with in the valley? Dead bodies. Corpses lying around. I see people do that all the time. They're happy something happened but then they don't move past the first phase. "Hey, they've got flesh and skin and everything. And they got up and they came together! We've never seen anything like this!" Yeah, but they're still dead. That is not good enough. Then they say, "Well, it's better than it was. Things are a little better." I can just hear them. "Come look at my valley of dead bodies. It's better than the loose bones." Well, that's not so great because those bodies are still dead and soon that flesh on them will start to stink, and before long we'll have just bones again!

Let's look at phase two of this passage. "Then said he unto me, Prophesy unto the wind, prophesy, son of man, and say to the wind, Thus saith the Lord GOD; Come from the four winds, O breath, and breathe upon these slain, that they may live." God never does things halfway. But He will test us to see if we'll do the first part before He gives us the next part. Ezekiel prophesied and breath came into those bodies. They came to life and stood on their feet, an exceedingly great army. There are too many times people get through phase one and they're real happy. We are all happy when we see God do something.

But we have not seen ALL that God wants to do. He wants us to continue on until there is wholeness and fullness of life. We must not stop until we have allowed God to complete His work.

As I said previously, the Lord tells us in His Word that we need to deal with the "mountains" in our lives. Mountains represent problems or obstacles. In Ezekiel 35, the Lord speaks to Ezekiel and says to him, "Son of man, set your face against Mount Seir and prophesy against it" (verse 2). Notice he's prophesying to a mountain. God wants you to understand you must set your face against the mountain—the problem, the obstacle—and speak to it.

We see again in chapter 36 the Lord tells Ezekiel to prophesy to the mountains of Israel. God's people had been dispersed and the enemies of Israel had taken possession of the mountains. The mountains had become desolate wastelands. The mountains were "unclean" from the residue of the heathen in the land (verse 3). God called Ezekiel to prophesy and proclaim that His people would walk upon and inhabit those mountains once again. Those mountains belonged to Israel. They belonged to God's people. But God had Ezekiel prophesy and call those mountains back to life and to become fruitful "like the garden of Eden" (verse 35). Do you have a desolate place in your life? Is there an "unclean mountain" that is hindering God's blessings in your life? Then prophesy to it! Speak to it in the Name of the Lord! It has ears. Everything has ears. Prophesy and speak the Word of the Lord concerning the desolate areas of your life. In Ezekiel 36:8 the Lord said, "But ye, O mountains of Israel, ye shall shoot forth your branches, and yield your fruit..." Prophesy that the desolate areas in your life will no longer be desolate but they shall come to life and become fruitful! Glory to God!!!

Chapter 8

PROPHESY, DECLARE, AND GET READY FOR RAIN!

THROUGHOUT THE BIBLE we see how God used people to speak His Word in power and authority to change situations and circumstances. In 1 Kings 17 we find how God used His prophet Elijah. In obedience to God, Elijah said to King Ahab, "There shall not be dew nor rain these years, but according to my word" (1 Kings 17:1). In other words, "It's not going to rain until I say so." After three years of no rain and great famine in the land, the Word of the Lord came to Elijah saying "Go show yourself to Ahab, and I will send rain upon the earth" (1 Kings 18:1). The Spirit of the Lord came upon Elijah and he went straight to the King and told him what God had said. Elijah could have said to himself, "Well, what if I do that and then it doesn't rain and I make a fool of myself?" But he didn't do that. He was fully persuaded that what God had told him would come to pass. He told Ahab to hurry up and eat and drink and then run for cover because, as he put it, "There is a sound of abundance of rain" (verse 41). It wasn't Elijah who said rain was coming; it was God speaking through him. God had given him the word, but Elijah had to be bold enough to say what God had said. He had to be bold enough to tell the king "rain is coming" even though there was not a cloud in the sky.

After he delivered the word to King Ahab, Elijah went up on the mountain and prayed. Then he told his servant:

> Go up now, look toward the sea. And he went up, and looked, and said, There is nothing. And he said, Go again seven times. And it came to pass at the seventh time, that he said, Behold, there ariseth a little cloud out of the sea, like a man's hand. And he said, Go up, say unto Ahab, Prepare thy chariot, and get thee down that the rain stop thee not. And it came to pass in the mean while, that the heaven was black with clouds and wind, and there was a great rain.
>
> —1 KINGS 18:43–45

Seven times Elijah sent his servant to go and look. Some of us would have quit after the first or second time. We would be thinking, "This isn't working," and then we would have quit. You know why we would have quit? Because we'd be *trying* God instead of *proving* God. But Elijah was proving the Word of the Lord. "There's nothing there." "Well, go look again." "But there's nothing there." "Go look again." Finally, they saw a cloud about the size of a man's hand. The servant could have said, "Well, don't we want to wait and see if anything develops? It may not stay, you know. That one little cloud could get blown away." Elijah didn't need to see raindrops before he would believe rain was coming. He had the Word of God. He knew it was going to rain, not just a sprinkle but buckets. And rain it did!

Maybe it looks like there will never be any "rain" in your life again. Maybe you can't see any sign that God is working on your behalf. You may be saying, "We're living in hard times. There are no jobs." Go look again. "We're living in difficult times. No one has any money." Go look again. "The doctor says there is no help for me." Go look again. Do like Elijah did. Speak God's Word. Prove His Word. Get ready for the rain!

You and I are righteous, justified, bought with the Blood of Jesus. We are filled with the Holy Spirit of God. The Holy Spirit—the power of God, the power of creation—lives in you. Nevertheless, it's possible for God to live in you and yet you not honor Him. What does that mean? It means that we do not give Him first place in our lives. If that's the case, then we have too much of what the world has taught us and too much of our own experiences influencing our thinking. These things hinder our faith and trust in God. We are prevented from giving Him first place and honor in our lives. We can never rise above our concept of God. We can never fully believe and trust His Word if we do not believe and trust in Him and His goodness. If we do not fully trust Him and His Word, we may have a tendency to say, "Well, I know the Bible says that, *but*..." instead of saying, "The Bible says this, and bless God that is what I believe! It's going to be the way the Bible says!" Or we may have a tendency to say, "Well, you know, that's just the way it is. That's the way it goes."

The truth is God is on our side. God is not mad with us. He only wants good things for us. We have to learn that it does not have to be the way "they" say. Things are not what they appear to be. That situation can change! It can change for your good. How do you make that happen? Grab hold of the Word of God and don't turn it loose! Keep going before God, saying, "Your Word says," then tell Him exactly what His Word says. In other words, put Him in remembrance of His Word. Tell the Lord, "Let's you and I reason together. I found the promise in Your Word and I am not going to be denied!" Argue your case before Him. Then begin to prophesy. Call things to be the way you want them to be, not the way they currently are. Call those things that be not as though they were and watch them come to pass. Call dead things back to life again. You can do that because you are filled with the very life of God. Life speaks life. You call it into being in the Name of the Lord!

God is saying to us, "Put me in remembrance of My Word. Plead your case based on what I have already said. Come on! Argue your case! Prove My Word! State it the way I stated it, and you'll see marvelous things happen!" Let's take God at His Word! Prophesy and prove God!

pronounce speak utter

Prophetic Declarations

proclaim

prophesy declare

say decree

You shall declare a thing, and it will be established for you.
Job 22:28

DECLARATIONS FOR PROVING GOD

We have seen clearly that God has an expectation of us. He expects us to come boldly before His throne and present our case to Him. In order for us to be able to do that we must know what His Word says so that we know we are in line with His will. As we state our case, or reason with God, we prophesy; we speak forth His Word in faith and confidence that He is overseeing it to perform it. Say to yourself, "I am going to prophesy! I am going to prove God! He will oversee His Word and perform it. I can be, have, and do everything God says I can." Once we do that we have a right to expect God to perform His Word and bring it to pass in our lives.

To help you begin to operate in this, you'll find in this section declaration statements based on God's Word organized according to topic. These are not direct quotations from the Bible but are paraphrased confessions of the scriptures. At the end of each section, some of the statements are combined into paragraph form as an example to you in forming your own declarations.

Prophesy God's Word over your life, standing in faith, believing you will see it come to pass. Go ahead...step out boldly in faith and speak the Word of God. Proclaim His will for your life. Prophesy and prove God!

CHILDREN

I cherish my children because they are a gift from the Lord, and they are a reward to me. [Psalm 127:3]

Because my children are being trained up in the way they should go (according to God's ways), they will not depart from it. [Proverbs 22:6]

Because I walk in the fear of the Lord and have strong confidence in Him, my children shall have a place of refuge. [Proverbs 14:26]

Because I hear and observe the words of the Lord and do that which is good and right in His sight, it goes well with me and with my children. [Deuteronomy 12:28]

The Lord will pour out His Spirit and His blessings upon my children. [Isaiah 44:3]

The Lord gives His angels charge over my children to keep and guard them in all their ways. [Psalm 91:11]

Because my children obey and honor their parents, they will live long. [Ephesians 6:1–3]

All my children are taught by the Lord and great is their peace. [Isaiah 54:13]

The Lord will fight those who fight with me, and He will save my children. [Isaiah 49:25]

I declare that my children are a gift to me and a blessing of the Lord. My children are trained up in the ways of the Lord and when they are older they will not depart from His ways. I prophesy that as for me and my household, we will serve the Lord all the days of our lives. Because I am in covenant relationship with God, the enemy is turned away from my children. The Spirit of the Lord and His blessings are poured out upon my children. The Lord has given His angels to watch over, guard, and protect my children and to preserve them in the ways of the Lord.

CHILDREN (BARRENNESS)

Children are a heritage of the Lord; therefore, they are my heritage and my reward. [Psalm 127:3]

The Lord has made me to be like a fruitful vine, producing many children. [Psalm 128:3]

Christ has redeemed me from the curse which includes barrenness. [Galatians 3:13]

Because I listen diligently to the voice of the Lord and am a doer of His Word, my womb is blessed and productive. [Deuteronomy 28:1]

The Lord has made me to be a joyful mother of children. [Psalm 113:9]

Because I delight myself in the Lord, He gives me the desires of my heart, which includes children. [Psalm 37:4]

God will bless me with the blessings of the womb. [Genesis 49:25]

God's Word says His people are blessed above all people and there shall be no barren among us. [Deuteronomy 7:14]

I decree and prophesy that I am in right standing and covenant relationship with God. I have been redeemed from the curse of barrenness. I am blessed, fruitful, and productive and my children shall be many in the earth to glorify God. My God is faithful. He shall oversee His Word to perform it and bring it to pass. My God shall give me children because they are the desire of my heart.

COMFORT

In the multitude of my anxious thoughts within me, the Lord comforts and cheers and delights my soul! [Psalm 94:19]

The Comforter (the Holy Spirit) abides with me and brings me comfort at all times. [John 14:16]

Whenever I find myself in mourning, I can turn to the Lord and know that He will comfort me. [Matthew 5:4]

My God is the God of all comfort. He comforts (consoles and encourages) me in every trouble so that I may be able to comfort those which are in any trouble, with the comfort with which I have been comforted. [2 Corinthians 1:3–4]

The Lord is my Shepherd. Even when I walk through the darkest valley I will not be afraid, for He is close beside me. His rod of protection and His staff of guidance protect and comfort me. [Psalm 23:4]

My Lord comforts me on every side. [Psalm 71:21]

God has promised me that His unfailing love will comfort me. [Psalm 119:76]

The Lord is my Shepherd. He has promised He will never leave or forsake me. Whenever I find myself in mourning, I can turn to the Lord and know that He will comfort me. He is the God of all comfort. In the midst of trials, troubles, or disappointments He consoles, encourages, and strengthens me with His unfailing love.

COURAGE / ENCOURAGEMENT

I can do all things through Christ who strengthens me. [Philippians 4:13]

I am of good courage, and the Lord strengthens my heart. [Psalm 31:24]

Even though I walk in the midst of trouble, God revives me. The Lord stretches forth His hand against the wrath of my enemy, and His right hand saves me. [Psalm 138:7]

The Lord will grant me, according to the riches of His glory, to be strengthened with might by His Spirit. [Ephesians 3:16]

My soul waits for the Lord. In the midst of trouble, He is my help and my shield. [Psalm 33:20]

The Lord my God will hold my right hand, saying to me, "Fear not. I will help you." [Isaiah 41:13]

I will hearken to the Word of the Lord who says to me, "Be not afraid nor dismayed…for the battle is not yours, but God's." [2 Chronicles 20:15]

I shall hope in my God and I shall praise Him who is the health of my countenance. [Psalm 42:11]

The Lord is a shield for me. He is my glory and the lifter up of my head. [Psalm 3:3]

I will not fear, for my God is with me. I will not be discouraged, for He is my God. He will strengthen me and help me. He will uphold me with His victorious right hand. [Isaiah 41:10]

The Lord is my light and my salvation; whom shall I fear? The Lord is the strength of my life; of whom shall I be afraid? [Psalm 27:1]

I praise God for His Word. I trust in Him, so why should I be afraid? What can mere mortals do to me? [Psalm 56:4]

God is my salvation. I will trust in Him, and I will not be afraid. The Lord is my strength and my song. He has given me the victory. [Isaiah 12:2]

If God be for me, who can be against me? [Romans 8:31]

God has not given me a spirit of fear, but of power and love and of a sound mind. [2 Timothy 1:7]

No weapon formed against me shall prosper. Every tongue which rises against me, the Lord will condemn. [Isaiah 54:17]

I declare that God has not given me a spirit of fear. He has given me the Holy Spirit which is the Spirit of power and of love and of a sound mind. I am more than a conqueror in this life and I can do all things through the power and strength of the Lord Jesus. When need arises, I come boldly before the throne of grace and there I find mercy and receive all the help I need. I walk in favor with God and man. I boldly proclaim that if God be for me, who or what can be against me? I am surrounded by the goodness and mercy of God, and they follow me all the days of my life!

FAITH

I have faith in God! [Mark 11:22]

I walk by faith and not by sight. [2 Corinthians 5:7]

The life which I now live I live by the faith of the Son of God, who loved me and gave Himself for me. [Galatians 2:20]

My faith is the substance of things I hope for; it is the evidence of things I have not yet seen. [Hebrews 11:1]

As I hear the Word of God, my faith is increased. [Romans 10:17]

My faith is not in the wisdom of men but in the power of God. [1 Corinthians 2:5]

I know that all things are possible to me because I believe. [Mark 9:23]

My faith has made me whole. [Luke 17:19]

Because I am just (made righteous by the Blood of Jesus), I live by faith. [Romans 1:17]

I have boldness and access to God through faith in Jesus. [Ephesians 3:12]

I walk in faith, a fruit of the Spirit. [Galatians 5:22]

I have not been justified by the works of the law but by faith in Christ. [Galatians 2:16]

I am justified by faith, apart from the works of the law. [Romans 3:28]

I have the same Spirit of faith as he who wrote, "I have believed and therefore have I spoken." I too believe, and therefore I speak. [2 Corinthians 4:13]

If I have faith and do not doubt, and if I believe those things which I say will be done, I can say to the mountain (obstacle or problem), "Be removed and cast into the sea," and I will have what I say. Whatever things I ask for, as I pray I believe that I receive them, and therefore I know that I have what I have asked for. [Mark 11:23–24]

Just like Abraham, I do not waver in unbelief, and I am strengthened in faith, giving glory to God. [Romans 4:20]

I've been justified by faith and have peace with God through Jesus Christ, through whom I have access by faith into God's grace. [Romans 5:1–2]

God answers my prayers as I have believed. [Matthew 8:13]

I fight the good fight of faith and lay hold on eternal life. [1 Timothy 6:12]

My faith, trust, hope, and confidence are in God. I'm not moved by what I see, only by what I believe. I believe all things are possible with God. My faith is the very substance and evidence of everything I desire and need. I believe that when I pray, I receive according to my faith. The life which I live, I live by the faith of the Son of God who loved me and gave Himself for me. Because I am just (made righteous by the Blood of Jesus), I

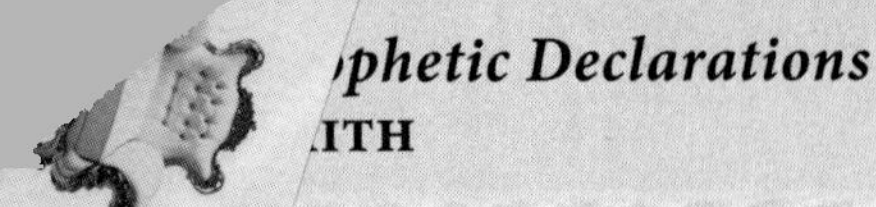

…h. If I have faith and do not doubt, I can say to the mount… (obstacle or problem), "Be removed and cast into the sea." I do not waver in unbelief. I am strengthened in faith, giving glory to God.

Faithfulness of God

God who has promised is faithful to me. [Hebrews 10:23]

God is a faithful God and keeps covenant and mercy with me because I love Him and keep His commandments. [Deuteronomy 7:9]

God is faithful to His Word. His covenant with me He will not break, nor alter that which has gone forth from His mouth. [Psalm 89:34]

God cannot lie. Therefore, I can rely on His Word. He has spoken and shall do what He has spoken. [Numbers 23:19]

The Lord is faithful. He will establish me and keep me from evil. [2 Thessalonians 3:3]

The God of peace Himself sanctifies me completely. My whole spirit, soul, and body are preserved sound and complete and blameless. Faithful is He who called me who also will do it. [1 Thessalonians 5:23–24]

There shall not one word fail of all God's good promises. [1 Kings 8:56]

Jesus is a merciful and faithful High Priest in things pertaining to God to make atonement for my sins. [Hebrews 2:17]

If I confess my sins, the Lord is faithful and just to forgive me my sins and cleanse me from all unrighteousness. [1 John 1:9]

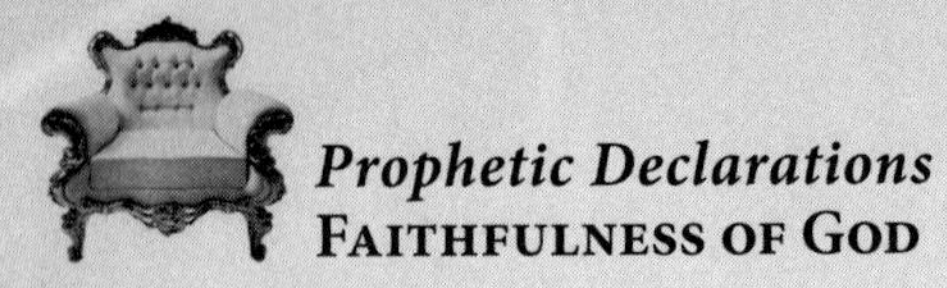

God is faithful to me. He establishes me and keeps me from evil. Because I love Him and keep His commandments, He keeps covenant and mercy with me. His covenant with me He will not break. I can rely on Him to be faithful to His Word. There shall not one Word fail of all of God's promises to me. God, who is faithful, sanctifies me completely, and my spirit, soul, and body are preserved sound and complete and blameless.

FINANCES / PROSPERITY / PROVISION

Because I meditate upon God's Word and do His Word, my way is prosperous and I have good success. [Joshua 1:8]

The Lord desires that I prosper and be in health, even as my soul prospers. [3 John 2]

I am blessed because I fear the Lord and delight greatly in His commandments. My descendants will be mighty on the earth. Wealth and riches are in my house, and my righteousness endures forever. [Psalm 112:1–3]

I will earnestly remember the Lord my God, for it is He who gives me power to get wealth, that He may establish His covenant. [Deuteronomy 8:18]

I will magnify the Lord who has pleasure in and delights in my prosperity. [Psalm 35:27]

I know that if I pay my tithes, the Lord will open the windows of Heaven and pour me out a blessing that there shall not be room enough to receive it. And He will rebuke the devourer of my finances. [Malachi 3:10–11]

The Lord supplies all my need according to His riches in glory by Christ Jesus. [Philippians 4:19]

Because I am a giver, men give to me in abundance—good measure, pressed down, shaken together, and running over. [Luke 6:38]

The Lord is my Shepherd (to feed, guide, protect, and provide for me). I will never be in lack. [Psalm 23:1]

My God will liberally supply all my needs from His glorious riches which have been given to me in Christ Jesus. [Philippians 4:19]

I will not be anxious concerning food and drink and clothes and other essentials. My heavenly Father knows that I have need of these things. I will instead seek above all else the Kingdom of God and His righteousness, and then all these things will be added to me. [Matthew 6:31–33]

God makes all grace come to me in abundance so that I will always have all that I need and plenty left over to share with others. [2 Corinthians 9:8]

I know that my God, considering He did not spare even His own Son but gave Him up for me, will freely and graciously give me all things I need. [Romans 8:32]

Because I fear and reverence the Lord, I will always have all that I need. Because I seek the Lord, I will not want any good thing. [Psalm 34:9–10]

Through Jesus Christ God has blessed me with the same blessing He promised to Abraham so that by faith I might receive the promise of the Spirit. [Galatians 3:14]

I hear and receive the seed of God's Word and it brings a harvest of thirty, sixty, some a hundred times what was sown. [Mark 4:20]

When I am generous, I increase more. When I withhold what is fitting or justly due, it results in lack. When I give to others, I get richer. When I help others, I am myself helped. [Proverbs 11:24–25]

Abraham was rich in cattle, silver, and gold. Because the blessing of Abraham rests upon me, I too am rich. [Genesis 13:2]

I honor the Lord with my possessions, and with the firstfruits of all my increase. [Proverbs 3:9]

The blessing of the Lord makes me rich, and He adds no sorrow with it. [Proverbs 10:22]

God desires that I prosper. I am redeemed from the curse of poverty and lack. Since I bring my tithe into God's House, He opens the windows of Heaven and pours out for me a blessing my storehouse cannot contain. I have sown my seed, and I will have a thirty, sixty, even a one hundred fold return. God said if I would give, it would be given unto me, good measure, pressed down, and shaken together. I will never be poor. My God supplies all my needs according to His riches in glory. I have plenty to help the needs of others, and much more to put in store. The blessings of the Lord overtake me. I believe I receive unexpected sources of income and miracle cancellations of debt. Because God delights in my prosperity, wealth and riches are in my house forever!

FORGIVENESS

The Lord is good and ready to forgive and plentiful in mercy for me when I call upon Him. [Psalm 86:5]

I know that if I forgive others their sins, my Father in Heaven will forgive my sins. [Mark 11:25–26]

When I confess my sins, God is faithful and just to forgive me and cleanse me from all unrighteousness. [1 John 1:9]

I make the decision to forgive others just as God has forgiven me, even when I know I don't deserve His forgiveness. [Matthew 6:12]

In Jesus, I have redemption through His Blood and the forgiveness of my sins according to the riches of His grace. [Ephesians 1:7]

My sins are forgiven me for His Name's sake. [1 John 2:12]

I am kind and forgiving of others because God in Christ forgave me. [Ephesians 4:32]

I bless those who curse me and I pray for those who spitefully use me. [Luke 6:28]

I keep no record of wrongs done to me. [1 Corinthians 13:5]

I reconcile myself to those who have anything against me. [Matthew 5:24]

I bless them which persecute me. [Romans 12:14]

I forgive every one that is indebted to me. [Luke 11:4]

The Lord is good, kind, and merciful to me. He has forgiven me all of my sins and trespasses. Because God has graciously forgiven me I must forgive others. I keep no record of wrongs done to me. I will pray for and bless those who persecute or harm me. I choose to walk in love and forgiveness toward others.

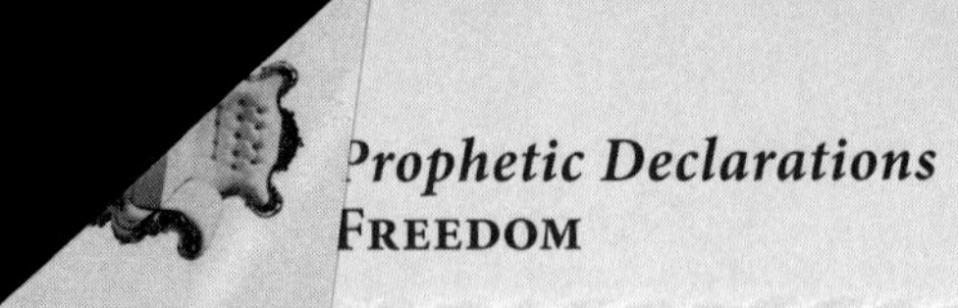

FREEDOM

Because I read and study God's Word, I know the truth, and the truth has made me free. [John 8:32]

I am in Christ and therefore a new creation; old things have passed away and all things are made new. [2 Corinthians 5:17]

I will stand fast in the liberty with which Christ has made me free, and I will not again be entangled with the yoke of bondage. [Galatians 5:1]

The Son has made me free; therefore, I am free indeed. [John 8:36]

Sin shall not have dominion over me, for I am no longer under the law, but under grace. [Romans 6:14]

There is no longer any condemnation to me because I am in Christ Jesus and I walk not after the flesh but after the Spirit. For the law of the Spirit of life in Christ Jesus has made me free from the law of sin and death. [Romans 8:1–2]

Because I walk in the Spirit, I will not fulfill the lusts of the flesh. [Galatians 5:16]

Because my steps are ordered in God's Word, He will not allow iniquity to have dominion over me. [Psalm 119:133]

The Lord is my deliverer. [Psalm 18:2]

I am no longer in bondage to sin but am a servant of righteousness. [Romans 6:18]

The Lord has delivered my soul in peace from the battle that was against me. [Psalm 55:18]

The truth of God's Word has made me free from every bondage of the enemy. I am a new creation in Christ and old things have passed away. I am no longer in bondage to sin but am a servant of righteousness. There is now no condemnation toward me, for I have the grace of God. Because I walk in the Spirit, I will not fulfill the lusts of the flesh. He has delivered my soul in peace from the battle that was against me. Because the Son has made me free, I am free indeed!

GIVING / GENEROSITY

I know that because I sow bountifully I shall reap bountifully. Because I am a cheerful giver, God is able to make all grace abound toward me, that I always having all sufficiency in all things may abound to every good work. [2 Corinthians 9:6–8]

I lay up for myself treasures in Heaven, where neither moth nor rust does corrupt, and where thieves do not break through nor steal. I know that where my treasure is, there will my heart be also. [Matthew 6:19–21]

Because I am a giver, men shall give to me, pressed down, shaken together, and running over. [Luke 6:38]

When I am generous, I increase more. When I withhold what is fitting or justly due, it results in lack. When I give to others, I get richer. When I help others, I am myself helped. [Proverbs 11:24–25]

God will make me rich in every way so that I can be generous and my generosity will bring forth thanksgiving to God. [2 Corinthians 9:11]

Because I am noble, openhearted, and liberal, I devise noble things. I stand for what is noble, openhearted, and generous. [Isaiah 32:8]

I don't neglect or refuse to extend hospitality to strangers in the brotherhood, being friendly, cordial, and gracious, sharing the comforts of my home and doing my part generously. [Hebrews 13:2]

I do good, am rich in good works, and liberal and generous of heart, and ready to share with others. [1 Timothy 6:18]

Because I deal generously and lend, and conduct my affairs with justice, it is well with me. [Psalm 112:5]

Because I am merciful, kind, and generous, my deeds return to bless me. [Proverbs 11:17]

I stand for what is noble, openhearted, and generous. I am merciful, kind, liberal and of a generous heart, giving to others liberally. God gives all things to me liberally and I in turn give to others. I lay up for myself treasures in Heaven and there my heart is also. My generosity and giving bring forth thanksgiving and glory to God. Because I give, I shall receive back good measure, pressed down, and shaken together and running over. I am a cheerful giver. God makes all grace abound toward me so I have sufficiency in all things and I am enriched in all things and in every way so that I can be generous to others.

GRACE

There is now no condemnation toward me because I am in Christ Jesus. [Romans 8:1]

By His grace through redemption in Christ Jesus, I am justified and made upright and in right standing with God. [Romans 3:24]

Sin shall not have dominion over me, for I am not under the law, but under grace. [Romans 6:14]

I can come boldly to the throne of grace and obtain mercy and find grace to help in time of need. [Hebrews 4:16]

Because of my faith, Christ has brought me into this place of undeserved privilege where I now stand, and I confidently and joyfully look forward to sharing God's glory. [Romans 5:2]

The Lord gives grace and glory. Because I walk uprightly before Him, no good thing will He withhold from me. [Psalm 84:11]

God makes all grace (every favor and earthly blessing) abound toward me, causing me to have enough of everything—enough to give to every good work. [2 Corinthians 9:8]

From His abundance, I receive one gracious blessing after another. [John 1:16]

There is no longer any condemnation toward me whatsoever! I can come boldly to the throne of God's grace and obtain mercy and find grace to help in time of need. The Lord gives grace and glory. Because I walk uprightly before Him, no good thing will He withhold from me. From His abundance, I receive one gracious blessing after another. Christ has brought me into this place of undeserved privilege where I now stand, and I confidently and joyfully look forward to sharing God's glory!

GRATITUDE AND THANKFULNESS

I will give thanks unto the Lord, for He is good; His mercy endures forever. [Psalm 107:1]

I will proclaim with the voice of thanksgiving and tell of all His wondrous works. [Psalm 26:7]

I will give thanks always for all things to God the Father in the Name of our Lord Jesus Christ. [Ephesians 5:20]

I will give thanks in everything because I know that is the Lord's will for me in all situations. [1 Thessalonians 5:18]

The Lord has turned my mourning into joyful dancing. He has taken away my clothes of mourning and clothed me with joy, that I might sing praises to Him and not be silent. I will give Him thanks forever! [Psalm 30:11–12]

I through Jesus offer a continual sacrifice of praise to God, giving thanks to His Name. [Hebrews 13:15]

I enter His gates with thanksgiving and His courts with praise. I am thankful to Him and I praise His Name. For the Lord is good. His unfailing love continues forever, and His faithfulness continues for all generations. [Psalm 100:4–5]

I sing praises to the Lord, and I give thanks at the remembrance of His Holy Name. [Psalm 30:4]

I will bless the Lord with my soul and all that is within me, I will bless His holy name and I will not forget all His benefits. [Psalm 103:1–2]

I am not anxious or worried. I pray and ask God for all that I need, always giving thanks to Him. [Philippians 4:6]

I raise my voice in praise and thanksgiving and tell of His wondrous works. [Psalm 26:7]

I will sing to Him and not be silent. I will give thanks to Him forever. [Psalm 30:12]

I give thanks to the Lord because God says it is a good and delightful thing. [Psalm 92:1]

I make thankfulness my sacrifice to God. [Psalm 50:14]

I give blessing and glory and wisdom and thanksgiving and honor and power and might to my God. [Revelation 7:12]

I give thanks unto the Lord because He is good and His mercy endures forever. I will proclaim with a voice of thanksgiving and tell of all His wondrous works. His mercies are fresh and new for me every morning. I bless the Lord will all my soul and I do not forget that daily He loads me with benefits. I am not anxious or worried about anything because I make my requests known to God with praise and thanksgiving. I offer the sacrifice of praise to the Lord and I will continually give thanks to His wondrous Name!

HEALING

The Lord Jesus bore my sicknesses and carried my pains; therefore, I don't have to carry them, and I will not carry them. They cannot stay in my body. [Isaiah 53:4]

He was wounded for my transgressions and bruised for my iniquities. The chastisement for me to obtain peace (wholeness) was upon Him, and by His stripes I am healed. [Isaiah 53:5]

The Lord has forgiven all my iniquities, and He has healed all my diseases. [Psalm 103:3]

The Lord has redeemed my life from destruction; therefore no sickness, no disease, no infirmity can destroy me. [Psalm 103:4]

The Lord sent His Word and healed me and delivered me from all destruction. [Psalm 107:20]

I pay attention to God's Word and listen with spiritual ears so that His Word penetrates deep into my heart. His Word brings life to me and healing to my whole body. [Proverbs 4:20–22]

My God has said that He is the Lord who heals me. Therefore, I believe Him to be my healer. [Exodus 15:26]

Christ has redeemed me from the curse of the law; therefore, I am redeemed from the effects of the curse which include sickness and disease. [Galatians 3:13]

I will live and not die, and I will declare the wonderful works of God in my life. [Psalm 118:17]

The Lord comes with healing, curing the incurable. [Jeremiah 30:17]

I declare that through Jesus I have been sanctified and made whole— spirit, soul, and body. [1 Thessalonians 5:23]

In life there are many afflictions, but the Lord delivers me out of them all. [Psalm 34:19]

The Lord revives me by His Word. [Psalm 119:25]

The Lord preserves me and keeps me alive. [Psalm 41:2]

Since the Spirit of Him who raised Jesus from the dead lives in me, He will give life to my body when it is sick or weak, and He will raise me up from that affliction. [Romans 8:11]

I trust in the Lord with my whole heart. I do not lean on my own understanding. In all my ways, I acknowledge Him and allow Him to direct my paths. I refuse to be wise in my own eyes, and I turn entirely from evil. Because of my continual trust in the Lord, my body glows with health, and my bones vibrate with life. [Proverbs 3:5–8]

I allow my mind and heart to be calm and undisturbed, and that brings life and health to my body. [Proverbs 14:30]

My merry heart is like medicine and my cheerful mind works healing. [Proverbs 17:22]

Jesus Himself bore my sins in His own body on the tree, making me become dead to sins and alive unto righteousness; and by His stripes I was healed. [1 Peter 2:24]

Jesus, Who was anointed by God with the Holy Spirit and power, went around doing good and healing all that were oppressed of the devil. Great multitudes followed Him, and He healed them all. Jesus is the same yesterday, and today, and forever. Therefore, He does those things in my life too! [Acts 10:38, Matthew 12:15, Hebrews 13:8]

Jesus came that I might have life and have it in abundance and in all its fullness. [John 10:10]

God works in me to will and to act in order to fulfill His good purpose in me. [Philippians 2:13]

With all boldness and confidence based on the power and authority of God's Word, I declare that I am healed. God has sent His Word and healed me. Jesus redeemed me from the curse of sin, sickness, and death. By the stripes of Jesus Christ I am healed! Jesus came to give me abundant life. I will live and not die and declare the wonderful works of God. I walk in divine health. There is nothing broken, missing, or lacking in me. The Word of God is life and health to all my flesh. Sickness and disease have no right to me. God will oversee His Word of healing to perform and bring it to pass. God works in me to fulfill His good purposes and plans. I am fully persuaded that I have health, healing, and abundant life in the Name of Jesus!

Honesty / Integrity

I will never steal, nor deceive, nor lie to others. [Leviticus 19:11]

I have a clear conscience, for I desire to walk uprightly and live a noble life, acting honorably and in complete honesty in all things. [Hebrews 13:18]

Because I am honest, I refuse to profit by fraud, I refuse to be bribed, I refuse to listen to those who plot bloodshed, and I close my eyes to evil. I will dwell on high and will be safe and protected. And I will never lack food, nor water. [Isaiah 33:15–16]

I treat others as I would have them treat me. [Matthew 7:12]

I have walked in integrity and have trusted in the Lord; therefore, I shall not slide backward. [Psalm 26:1]

I allow the Lord to teach me; therefore, I walk in truth. [Psalm 86:11]

I take heed to the Word of the Lord; therefore my way is pure, and my life is pure. [Psalm 119:9]

Because I abide in the Lord, I walk as He walked. [1 John 2:6]

The Lord upholds me in my integrity and sets me before His face forever. [Psalm 41:12]

My integrity guides me as I abide in the Lord, and I will walk as He walked. I never steal, deceive, or lie to others. Because I choose to be honest, I refuse to profit by fraud. I will not give in to bribery. I refuse to listen to those who plan to hurt anyone else and I will close my eyes to evil. I dwell on high and will be safe and protected. I treat others the way I want them to treat me. I walk in integrity and trust in the Lord. I take heed to the Word of God; therefore my way is pure.

HUMILITY

I am clothed with humility. God resists the proud, but because of my humility, I walk in the Lord's grace. [1 Peter 5:5]

Though the Lord be high, He has respect for me and brings me into fellowship with Him because I am lowly and humble. [Psalm 138:6]

Because I am humble, the Lord hears my desires and prepares my heart and causes His ear to hear me. [Psalm 10:17]

Because I am humble, the Lord will exalt me. [Matthew 23:12]

As one of God's chosen ones, purified and holy and well-beloved by God Himself, I clothe myself with tenderhearted pity and mercy, kind feeling, a lowly opinion of myself, gentle ways, and patience. [Colossians 3:12]

Because I walk in true humility, I have riches, honor, and long life. [Proverbs 22:4]

Because I humble myself and become like a little child (trusting, lowly, loving, forgiving), I am great in the Kingdom of Heaven. [Matthew 18:4]

Because I have a contrite and humble spirit, God dwells with me, and He revives my spirit and my heart. [Isaiah 57:15]

Because I humble myself before the Lord, He exalts me (lifts me up and makes my life significant). [James 4:10]

My soul boasts only in the Lord. [Psalm 34:2]

Because I am humble the Lord will exalt me. Because I am humble the Lord hears my desire and prepares my heart and causes His ear to hear me. As one of God's chosen ones, I clothe myself with tenderhearted pity and mercy, kind feeling, a lowly opinion of myself, gentle ways, and patience. As I humble myself and become like a little child I am great in the Kingdom of Heaven. Because I walk in the love of God, I humble myself before Him and I know that I shall prevail in life.

Intimacy and Fellowship with God

Because I "come unto Him," He gives me rest. [Matthew 11:28]

The Lord hides me in the secret place of His presence, and He keeps me from the plots of men and the strife of tongues. [Psalm 31:20]

Because I spend time in the Lord's presence, I have great joy and pleasure, and He shows me the path of life. [Psalm 16:11]

In rest and quietness before the Lord, and in trusting Him, I have strength and salvation. [Isaiah 30:15]

Because I draw near to God, He draws near to me. [James 4:8]

Because I diligently seek the Lord, He brings me reward. [Hebrews 11:6]

I was created for His pleasure, and He is worthy to receive all glory and all honor and all power. [Revelation 4:11]

As the deer pants and longs for the water brooks, I pant and long for my God. My inner self thirsts for the living God. [Psalm 42:1–2]

My great desire is that I may know Him. [Philippians 3:10]

Earnestly I seek the Lord. My inner self thirsts for Him. My flesh longs and is faint for Him. I look upon Him to see His power and His glory. Because His loving-kindness is better than life, my lips praise Him. I bless Him while I live. I lift my hands in His Name. My whole being is satisfied more than the richest feast, and my mouth praises Him with joyful lips. [Psalm 63:1–5]

Because I come unto the Lord, He gives me rest. I seek the Lord earnestly. My inner self thirsts for Him. My flesh longs for and faints for Him. I look upon Him and I see His power and His glory. Because His loving-kindness is better than life, my lips will praise Him. I will bless Him while I live. I lift my hands in His Name. My whole being is satisfied more than the richest feast and my mouth will praise Him with joyful lips.

Joy

I am glad in the Lord and rejoice and shout for joy! [Psalm 32:11]

I make a joyful noise unto the Lord and serve the Lord with gladness and come before His presence with singing. [Psalm 100:1–2]

My heart rejoices in the Lord. I have trusted in His holy Name. [Psalm 33:21]

I greatly rejoice IN the Lord. My soul is joyful in my God. For He has clothed me with the garments of salvation and covered me with the robe of righteousness. [Isaiah 61:10]

Even though I've never seen Him, I love Him. Though I've never seen Him, I believe in Him. And I rejoice with a joy that is inexpressible and full of glory. [1 Peter 1:8]

The Lord gives me beauty in place of ashes. He gives me the oil of joy in place of mourning. He gives me a garment of praise in place of the spirit of heaviness. And I am called a tree of righteousness, the planting of the Lord, that He may be glorified in my life. [Isaiah 61:3]

Because I put my trust in the Lord, I can rejoice and I can shout for joy because He defends me. [Psalm 5:11]

I have received atonement through Jesus Christ, and I joy in God through the Lord Jesus. [Romans 5:11]

Because the Lord is my strength and my shield and my heart trusts in Him, I am helped by Him; therefore, my heart greatly rejoices, and with my song I praise Him. [Psalm 28:7]

The joy of the Lord is my strength! [Nehemiah 8:10]

Because the Lord is my strength and my shield and my heart trusts in Him, I am helped by Him; therefore, my heart greatly rejoices, and with my song I praise Him. I put my trust in the Lord, therefore I can rejoice and shout for joy because He defends me. I have received atonement through Jesus Christ, and I joy in God through the Lord Jesus. I am glad in the Lord and rejoice in Him. My soul shall be joyful in my God, for He has clothed me with the garments of salvation and covered me with the robe of righteousness!

Love (God's Love for Me / My Love for Him)

God is love. Therefore, I know that God loves me. [1 John 4:8]

For God so loved me that He gave His only begotten Son. And because I believe in Him, I will not perish, but will have life eternal. [John 3:16]

The Lord loves me with an everlasting love and has drawn me to Himself with loving-kindness. [Jeremiah 31:3]

Neither death, nor life, nor angels, nor principalities, nor powers, nor things present, nor things to come, nor height, nor depth, nor any other creature can separate me from the love of God. [Romans 8:38–39]

God, who is rich in mercy, loves me with a great love. [Ephesians 2:4]

God loves me exactly the same as He loves Jesus. [John 17:23]

The Lord my God is with me, a Mighty One who saves me and gives me victory. He rejoices over me with gladness. He quiets me by His love. He rejoices over me with singing. [Zephaniah 3:17]

I have received the Spirit of adoption (the Spirit producing sonship) by which I cry Abba Father! [Romans 8:15]

I love the Lord my God with all my heart, with all my soul, with all my strength. [Deuteronomy 6:5]

I love you O Lord, my strength! [Psalm 18:1]

I have set my love upon Him; therefore, He delivers me, He rescues me, He sets me on high. [Psalm 91:14]

Because I love His Name, He looks upon me and is merciful to me. [Psalm 119:132]

God so loved me that He gave His own Son, Jesus, to purchase me and make me His own. The Lord loves me with an everlasting love and has drawn me to Himself. I can love Him because He first loved me. He loves me with an undying and incorruptible love. No thing or no one can ever separate me from the love of God. He is my ever present help. He watches over me at all times, He rejoices over me with singing. And because of His love, He gives me victory in every situation. Because I have set my love upon Him, He delivers me, He rescues me, He sets me on high!

Love (Love for Others)

I know how dearly God loves me, and He has given me His Holy Spirit to fill my heart with His love so I can love others. [Romans 5:5]

Because God first loved me, I have the capacity to love Him, and I choose to love others as Christ loves me. [1 John 4:19]

I love others with brotherly affection, taking delight in honoring others. [Romans 12:10]

I owe no man anything except to love him. [Romans 13:8]

I love others deeply from a pure heart. [1 Peter 1:22]

The Lord causes me to increase and abound in love toward others. He pours in His love so that it fills my life and splashes over on everyone around me. [1 Thessalonians 3:12]

Because God loves me, I love others. As I walk in love toward others, He abides in me, and His love is being perfected in me. [1 John 4:11–12]

I love others, for love is of God. [1 John 4:7]

Because Jesus said, "Love your neighbor," I walk in love toward others. [Matthew 22:39]

I let everything I do be done in love, true love to God and man as inspired by God's love for me. [1 Corinthians 16:14]

I let love for my fellow believers continue and be a fixed practice. I never let love fail. [Hebrews 13:1]

I imitate God in all that I do. I walk in love as Christ loved me and gave Himself up for me. [Ephesians 5:1–2]

Love causes me to do these things: I endure long and am patient and kind. I am not jealous or boastful or proud or rude. I don't demand my own way. I am not irritable. I keep no record of wrongs. I don't rejoice over injustice, but rejoice whenever the truth wins out. I never give up. I never lose faith. I am always hopeful and endure through every circumstance. Faith, hope, and love abide in me. But the greatest of these is love. [1 Corinthians 13:4–7, 13]

I know how dearly God loves me, and He has given me His Holy Spirit to fill my heart with His love so I can love others. Because God first loved me, I have the capacity to love Him, and I choose to love others as Christ loves me. I walk in love as Christ loved me and gave Himself up for me. I love others deeply from a pure heart. The Lord causes me to increase and abound in love toward others. I let everything be done in love (true love to God and man as inspired by God's love for me). He pours in His love so that it fills my life and splashes over on everyone around me!

LOVE (LOVE FOR SELF—HEALTHY SELF-ESTEEM)

I am God's masterpiece, created in Christ Jesus for good works which God prepared beforehand. [Ephesians 2:10]

I am fearfully and wonderfully made. [Psalm 139:14]

I have been adopted by my heavenly Father who I call "Abba" (my Daddy). [Romans 8:15]

I am a new creation in Christ. I have become a new person. The old life is gone. A new life has begun! [2 Corinthians 5:17]

I am chosen of God, holy and dearly loved. [Colossians 3:12]

I am a partaker of the divine nature and have been given exceedingly great and precious promises. [2 Peter 1:4]

I am chosen, and I am royalty. I am God's own possession. [1 Peter 2:9]

I was chosen in Christ before the foundation of the world. [Ephesians 1:4]

Before I can love others, I must love myself. My understanding of God's love for me shuts down any self-criticism. I am God's masterpiece created in Christ Jesus, and I am fearfully and wonderfully made. I am chosen of God, holy and dearly loved. I have been adopted by my heavenly Father, and through Jesus I have become a new person. The old life is gone. A new life has begun! God knows me better than I know myself. He is never mad with me. He loves me unconditionally with a boundless, magnificent love!

Marriage

I am subject in love to my spouse and my spouse is subject in love to me. [1 Peter 3:1]

I love my spouse as Christ loves the church and gave Himself for it. [Ephesians 5:25]

What God has joined together, no man will separate. [Mark 10:9]

I declare that my spouse and I walk in love. Therefore, we will never give up, never lose faith, always be hopeful, and endure through every circumstance. I declare that love never fails. [1 Corinthians 13:7–8]

My spouse and I are subject to one another out of reverence for Christ. [Ephesians 5:21]

We are kind to each other, tenderhearted toward one another, and forgiving of each other just as God through Christ has forgiven us. [Ephesians 4:32]

God gives us the power of patient endurance, He supplies encouragement, and He helps us to live in complete harmony with each other. [Romans 15:5]

My spouse and I accept each other just as Christ has accepted each of us. [Romans 15:7]

Because we are righteous, we conduct ourselves honorably and becomingly, not in quarreling and jealousy. [Romans 13:13]

Love is shed abroad in our hearts by the Holy Spirit. Because He is in us, we acknowledge that love reigns supreme. [Romans 5:5]

We live in mutual harmony and accord with one another delighting in each other, being of the same mind and united in spirit. [Philippians 2:2]

We seek peace, and it keeps our hearts in quietness and assurance. [Isaiah 32:17]

Our marriage is rooted and grounded in love. [Ephesians 3:17]

We are knit together in love and are made perfect for every good work to do God's will, who is working in us that which is pleasing in His sight. [Colossians 2:2, Colossians 1:10]

We continue our lives with each other in humility, gentleness, patience, bearing with one another in love, endeavoring to keep the unity of the Spirit in the bond of peace. [Ephesians 4:2–3]

My marriage is created by God and for the glory of God. My spouse and I love each other with the love of Christ Jesus which has been shed abroad in our hearts. My spouse and I live together in love and harmony because we care for each other in an honorable and becoming manner. My spouse and I are kind, gentle, compassionate and courteous to each other. Our marriage grows stronger and more Heaven-like each day because it is founded on God's Word and grounded in His love!

MERCY

For as the Heaven is high above the earth, so great is God's mercy toward me. [Psalm 103:11]

There is no god like my God, in Heaven above, or on earth beneath, who keeps covenant and mercy with me as I walk before Him with all my heart. [1 Kings 8:23]

My God is a God full of compassion, and gracious, long-suffering, and plenteous in mercy toward me. [Psalm 86:15]

The Lord will not remember the sins of my youth, nor my transgressions; but according to His mercy He will remember me for His goodness' sake. [Psalm 25:7]

The Lord will hear me and have mercy upon me; He is my helper. [Psalm 30:10]

I will be glad and rejoice in God's mercy; for He has seen my affliction and has known the distress of my soul. [Psalm 31:7]

In my time of need, I will come boldly to the throne of grace and obtain mercy and find help. [Hebrews 4:16]

I will do justly, love mercy, and walk humbly with my God. It is what the Lord requires of me. [Micah 6:8]

I will be merciful as my heavenly Father is merciful. [Luke 6:36]

I know that if I am merciful I will obtain mercy. [Matthew 5:7]

As I walk in mercy, I find favor and high esteem in the sight of God and man. [Proverbs 3:3–4]

Surely goodness and mercy and unfailing love shall follow me all the days of my life. [Psalm 23:6]

The Lord hears me and has mercy upon me because He is my helper. Because of God's mercy in my life, I am glad and I rejoice, for He has seen my affliction and has known the distresses of my soul. I walk in mercy toward others, and I will find favor and high esteem in the sight of God and man. Surely goodness and mercy and unfailing love shall follow me all the days of my life. As the Heaven is high above the earth, so great is God's mercy toward me. My God is a God full of compassion and gracious, long-suffering and plenteous in mercy toward me.

OBEDIENCE

The Lord my God will I serve, and His voice will I obey. [Joshua 24:24]

I am blessed because I hear the Word of God and put it into practice. [Luke 11:28]

Because I hear the Word of the Lord and do it, I am like a wise man that builds his house upon a rock. And that house will not fall even in the midst of torrential rains, massive floods, and strong winds. [Matthew 7:24–25]

Because I obey the voice of the Lord and keep His covenant, I am a special treasure to Him above all people. [Exodus 19:5]

Because I observe and hear the words of the Lord, and I do that which is good and right in the sight of the Lord, it will go well with me and with my children. [Deuteronomy 12:28]

Because I obey and serve the Lord, I shall spend my days in prosperity and my years in pleasantness. [Job 36:11]

I am a doer of the Word and not a hearer only. [James 1:22]

God's Word says that to obey is better than sacrifice. Therefore, I will please the Lord by walking in obedience to God and His Word. [1 Samuel 15:22]

I am a "doer" of the Word and not a hearer only. Because I hear the Word of the Lord and do it, I am like a wise man that builds his house on a rock. And when the storms of life come my way, I will not fail. I obey the voice of the Lord and keep His covenant. Because I obey the voice of the Lord and keep His commandments, I am a special treasure to Him. Because I choose to obey God and His Word I am pleasing to Him. Because I observe and hear the words of the Lord, and I do that which is good and right in His sight, it will go well with me and my children.

PATIENCE

Because I am a servant of the Lord, I am not quarrelsome but am gentle to all men, a teacher who is patient. [2 Timothy 2:24]

The testing of my faith works patience. In the midst of tests and trials, I will allow patience to have her perfect work, that I may be mature and complete, lacking nothing. [James 1:3–4]

I will walk in patience, a fruit of the Spirit. [Galatians 5:22]

I wait patiently on the Lord and I am of good courage. He strengthens my heart. [Psalm 27:14]

I hope for that which I do not see, and I wait for it with patience. [Romans 8:25]

I will never cast away my fearless confidence which has great compensation of reward. I will walk in patience, knowing that after having done the will of God, I will receive what He has promised. [Hebrews 10:35–36]

Because I hope in the Lord, my strength is renewed. I soar on wings like eagles, I run and will not grow weary, I walk and will not faint. [Isaiah 40:31]

I will not grow lazy (spiritually dull and indifferent) but will imitate those who through faith and patience inherit the promises. [Hebrews 6:12]

Because I am one of God's chosen, I clothe myself with compassion, kindness, humility, gentleness, and patience. [Colossians 3:12]

Love endures long and is patient. Because God's love works through me, I am patient. [1 Corinthians 13:4]

I consider it joy when I face trials, knowing that the testing of my faith produces patience. [James 1:2–3]

The Lord strengthens me with His own great power so that I will not give up when troubles come, but will be patient. [Colossians 1:11]

Because I am one of God's chosen, I clothe myself with compassion, kindness, humility, gentleness, and patience. Because God's love works through me, I am patient and I endure long. I consider every trial a joy because I know that the testing of my faith produces patience. Because I am a servant of the Lord, I am not quarrelsome but am gentle to all men, a teacher who is patient. The Lord strengthens me with His own great power so that I will not give up when trouble comes, but I will be patient.

PEACE

The peace of God which passes all understanding will guard my heart and mind through Jesus Christ. [Philippians 4:7]

The Lord will keep me in perfect peace because my mind is fixed on Him, trusting in Him. [Isaiah 26:3]

I will not let my heart be troubled or afraid. The Lord has given me His peace—not peace as the world gives, but it's *His* peace. [John 14:27]

The Lord of peace Himself gives me peace at all times in all ways, in all circumstances and in all conditions. [2 Thessalonians 3:16]

The Lord guides my feet into the path of peace. [Luke 1:79]

The Lord gives me strength and blesses me with peace. [Psalm 29:11]

Because my ways please the Lord, He makes even my enemies to be at peace with me. [Proverbs 16:7]

Having been justified by faith, I have peace with God through my Lord Jesus Christ. [Romans 5:1]

Because I love God's Word, I have great peace, and nothing shall cause me to stumble. [Psalm 119:165]

I know that the Kingdom of God is righteousness and peace and joy in the Holy Spirit. I will pursue after the things which make for harmony and peace and those things which edify others. [Romans 14:17–19]

Jesus is called the Prince of Peace. He lives in me; therefore, peace lives in me. [Isaiah 9:6]

Jesus was wounded for my transgressions, He was bruised for my iniquities. The chastisement for my peace was upon Him, and by His stripes I am healed. [Isaiah 53:5]

The God of love and peace is with me. [2 Corinthians 13:11]

In Jesus, I have perfect peace and confidence. [John 16:33]

My feet are fitted with the readiness that comes from the gospel of peace. [Ephesians 6:15]

God gives me more and more peace as I grow in the knowledge of God. [2 Peter 1:2]

God's wonderful favor and perfect peace give me freedom and liberty from all fears, anxieties, and conflicts. Grace and peace are multiplied to me through the knowledge of the Lord Jesus Christ, the very Prince of Peace. God guards me and keeps me in perfect peace because my mind is fixed on Him. As I grow in the knowledge of God, His peace is multiplied to me. I love and know God's Word; therefore nothing shall disturb my peace. God causes even my enemies to be at peace with me. God causes all things to work together for my good and welfare. God is my very source of peace and goodwill, the very Author and Promoter of peace.

PERSEVERANCE

I hold fast the profession of my faith without wavering; for He is faithful that promised. [Hebrews 10:23]

I strip off and throw aside every encumbrance and the sins which so easily entangle me. And I run with patient endurance and persistence the race that is set before me, looking away from all that will distract me and looking to Jesus, the Author and Finisher of my faith, Who for the joy of the prize that was set before Him endured the cross. [Hebrews 12:1–2]

If I hold my original confidence firm and steadfast to the end, then I am made a partaker of Christ and all that belongs to Him. [Hebrews 3:14]

I may be troubled, but I'm not distressed. I may be perplexed, but I'm not in despair. I may be persecuted, but I'm not forsaken. I may be knocked down, but I'm not knocked out. [2 Corinthians 4:8–9]

I will stand fast in the Lord. [Philippians 4:1]

I can do all things through Christ who strengthens me. [Philippians 4:13]

I will not grow weary in well-doing, for in due season I shall reap a harvest if I will not give up. [Galatians 6:9]

I do not become weary or lose heart in doing right but continue in well-doing without weakening. [2 Thessalonians 3:13]

I will not throw away my confident trust in the Lord which has great reward. [Hebrews 10:35]

I am invigorated and strengthened with all power according to the might of His glory to exercise every kind of endurance and patient perseverance with joy. [Colossians 1:11]

I persevere in every situation, every trial, every adversity. I stand fast in the Lord. I may be troubled, but I'm not distressed. I may be perplexed, but I'm not in despair. I may be persecuted, but I'm not forsaken. I may be knocked down, but I'm not knocked out. I hold fast the profession of my faith without wavering, for my God is faithful. I am strengthened by the Lord so that I do not grow weary or become fainthearted or lose my faith. I know that through my perseverance, others will see my faith in the Lord, and He will be glorified.

PRAISE

I will offer up the sacrifice of praise to God continually, giving thanks to His Name. [Hebrews 13:15]

I have been called to proclaim the praises of Him who has called me out of darkness into His marvelous light. [1 Peter 2:9]

I will greatly rejoice in the Lord. My soul shall be joyful in my God. [Isaiah 61:10]

Because His loving-kindness is better than life, my lips shall praise Him. I will bless Him while I live. I will lift up my hands in His Name. He satisfies me more than the richest feast. My mouth shall praise Him with joyful lips. [Psalm 63:3–5]

I will give thanks unto the Lord and call upon His Name. I will make known His deeds among the people. I will sing unto Him. I will talk of His wondrous works. I will glory in His holy Name. [Psalm 105:1–3]

While I live I will praise the Lord. I will sing praises to my God as long as I live and will sing praises to Him with my dying breath. [Psalm 146:2]

I will praise the Lord. It is good to sing praises to my God, for He is gracious and lovely, and praise is delightful and becoming. [Psalm 147:1]

I will clap my hands. I will shout unto God with the voice of triumph! [Psalm 47:1]

I will cause my mouth to be filled with His praise and with His honor all the day. [Psalm 71:8]

I will sing praises to God. I will sing praises to my King. For He is the King of all the earth, and I will sing to Him. [Psalm 47:6–7]

I will praise the Lord for His goodness and for His wonderful works in my life! [Psalm 107:8]

I offer up the sacrifice of praise to God continually. I greatly rejoice in the Lord. My soul is joyful in my God. Because His loving-kindness is better than life, my lips praise Him. I talk of His wondrous works. I glory in His holy Name. I praise the Lord for His goodness and for His wonderful works in my life. I sing praises to my King. For He is the King of all the earth, and I will sing to Him as long as I live.

PRAYER

Because I walk uprightly, my earnest, heartfelt prayer avails much, has great power and produces wonderful results. [James 5:16]

As I pray, I am believing that I am already receiving, and therefore I know I will have what I have asked. [Mark 11:24]

When I pray, if I have anything against anyone, I will forgive them so that my Father in Heaven will forgive me my sins. [Mark 11:25]

I know that if I ask anything according to His will, He hears me. And since I know that He hears my prayers, I know that I have that which I have requested. [1 John 5:14–15]

I rejoice in confident hope, I am patient in trouble, and I keep on praying. [Romans 12:12]

Because I keep on asking, I receive. Because I keep on seeking, I find. Because I keep on knocking, the door is opened to me. [Matthew 7:7]

As I live in Jesus, vitally united to Him, and His words live and remain in me, I ask for whatever I need, and I am granted my requests. [John 15:7]

I will call unto the Lord, and He will answer me and show me marvelous and wondrous things which I do not yet know. [Jeremiah 33:3]

I receive from Him whatever I ask because I obey Him and do the things that please Him. [1 John 3:22]

I will put God in remembrance of His Word, and I will state my case. [Isaiah 43:26]

I will not worry, but I will let my requests be unreservedly made known in the presence of God. [Philippians 4:6]

When two of us (believers) agree on something and ask according to God's will, it will be done for us by my Father in Heaven. [Matthew 18:19]

Whatever I ask in Jesus' Name will be granted. I will receive and my joy will be complete. [John 16:23–24]

When I don't know how to pray, the Spirit Himself makes intercession for me with groanings which cannot be uttered. The Spirit makes intercession for me according to the will of God. [Romans 8:26–27]

When I am in trouble, I will pray. When I am happy I will sing songs of praise. When I am sick, I will call the elders of the church to pray over me and anoint me with oil in the Name of the Lord. And those prayers will make me well and I will be raised up. I will confess my sins to others and pray for others so that I may be healed. [James 5:13–15]

The Lord, who in the exercise of His power that is at work within me, is able to do infinitely beyond all my highest prayers and thoughts. [Ephesians 3:20]

I have confidence (assurance, privilege of boldness) in Him that if I ask anything according to His will He listens and He hears me. [1 John 5:14]

The Lord Jesus says that if I ask anything in His Name, He will do it. [John 14:14]

When I think of the wisdom and scope of His plan, I fall down on my knees and pray to the Father. [Ephesians 3:14]

My earnest, heartfelt prayer avails much, has great power and produces wonderful results. As I pray, I believe that I receive, and I know I have what I have asked. I put God in remembrance of His Word and I state my case to Him. I do not worry but let my requests be unreservedly made known to Him. I remind myself that the Lord, who in the exercise of His power that is at work within me, is able to do infinitely beyond all my highest prayers and thoughts. The Lord gives me strength and fortitude to press in and press on in prayer, and He is making me into a prayer warrior.

PROTECTION

God is my refuge and my strength, a very present help in trouble. [Psalm 46:1]

The eternal God is my refuge, and His everlasting arms are underneath me. He shall thrust out the enemy from before me. [Deuteronomy 33:27]

The Lord is my defense and the rock of my refuge, my safe place. [Psalm 94:22]

The Lord is my rock, my fortress and my deliverer. In Him will I trust. He is my shield and the horn of my salvation, my high tower, and my refuge, my savior. He saves me from those who want to do me harm. I will call on the Lord who is worthy to be praised. So shall I be saved from my enemies. [2 Samuel 22:2–4]

Though I walk through the valley of the shadow of death, I will not fear; for my God is with me, His rod (to protect) and His staff (to guide) comfort me. [Psalm 23:4]

Because I have set my love upon the Lord, He will deliver me. He will set me on high because I know His Name (have a personal knowledge of His mercy, love, and kindness). I will call upon Him, and He will answer me. He will be with me in trouble and will deliver me and honor me. He will satisfy me with long life and will show me His salvation. [Psalm 91:14–16]

When I go through deep waters of trouble, my God is with me. When I pass through the rivers of oppression and adversity, they will not overflow me. When I walk through the fire of trial or tribulation, I will not be burned nor consumed. [Isaiah 43:2]

Because I listen to the Lord, I dwell in safety and will be secure without fear of evil. [Proverbs 1:33]

Because I dwell in the secret place of the Most High, I live under the shadow of the Almighty's protection. The Lord is my refuge and my fortress, and in Him I am safe. He is my God, and in Him do I trust. He will deliver me from the snares and traps of the enemy, and from deadly disease. He covers me with His feathers, and under His wings do I trust and find refuge. His truth is my shield. I will not be afraid because of the terror in the night, nor of the evil plots and fiery darts of the enemy that fly at me in the day, nor for the disease that walks in darkness, nor for the disaster that erupts at noonday. Even if a thousand fall at my side, and ten thousand at my right hand, it shall not come near me. [Psalm 91:1–7]

God has said that He will not in any way fail me nor give me up nor leave me without support. He will not in any degree leave me helpless nor abandon me nor let me down or relax His hold on me. [Hebrews 13:5]

No weapon formed against me shall prosper. [Isaiah 54:17]

The Lord is my rock, my fortress, my deliverer, and in Him do I trust. When I go through deep waters of trouble, my God is with me. When I pass through the rivers of oppression and adversity, they will not overflow me. When I walk through the fire of trial or tribulation, I will not be burned or consumed. Because I dwell in the secret place of the Most High, I live under the shadow of the Almighty's protection. God will not in any way fail me nor give me up nor leave me without support. He will not in any degree leave me helpless nor abandon me nor let me down nor relax His hold on me. God is my refuge and strength, a very present help in trouble. His everlasting arms are underneath me, undergirding me and keeping me safe. I can rest at ease knowing that He keeps careful watch over me, day and night.

RIGHTEOUSNESS

I have been made the righteousness of God in Christ Jesus. I'm not only right with God, but I am living a righteous life through Christ. [2 Corinthians 5:21]

Because I hunger and thirst after righteousness, I shall be filled with righteousness. [Matthew 5:6]

I am covered with a robe of righteousness. [Isaiah 61:10]

I have no righteousness of my own, but I have the righteousness that comes from trusting in Christ. For God's way of making me right with Him depends on my faith in Christ. [Philippians 3:9]

By the abundance of God's grace and His gift of righteousness through Christ, I will reign as a king in this life and triumph over sin and death. [Romans 5:17]

Because I walk uprightly and live in righteousness and speak truth in my heart, I will abide in the tabernacle of the Most High God. [Psalm 15:1–2]

Because I follow after righteousness and mercy, I find life, righteousness, and honor. [Proverbs 21:21]

I have been made the righteousness of God in Christ Jesus. I am no longer condemned but have become righteous in His sight. I am covered with a robe of righteousness. I have no righteousness of my own, but I have the righteousness that comes from trusting in Christ. By the abundance of God's grace and His gift of righteousness through Christ, I will reign as a king in this life and triumph over sin and death.

SALVATION

God's Word says that if I confess with my mouth the Lord Jesus and believe in my heart that God raised Him from the dead, I will be saved. Because I have done those things, I can declare that I am saved! [Romans 10:9]

I confirm that there is no other name under the heavens whereby we must be saved except the Name of Jesus. [Acts 4:12]

God so loved me that He gave His only begotten Son. Because I believe in the Son, I will not perish but have everlasting life. [John 3:16]

Because I have received Him, I am a child of God. [John 1:12]

Jesus became sin for me, that I might become the righteousness of God in Him. [2 Corinthians 5:21]

By grace I have been saved through faith, not of myself. It is the gift of God and not of works. [Ephesians 2:8]

God demonstrated His love for me in that while I was still a sinner, Christ died for me. [Romans 5:8]

Because I have been saved, I am a new creation. Old things have passed away and all things are made new. [2 Corinthians 5:17]

God gave His only begotten Son, Jesus, that if I would believe in Him and confess Him as my Lord, I would be saved. I believed and I confessed Him as Savior; therefore I am saved. All my sins are forgiven and I am a new creation in Christ. I walk uprightly before God and I will serve Him all the days of my life.

Note: If you have never been born again and entered into a relationship with God by accepting Jesus as your personal Lord and Savior, you can enter into that relationship with Him by praying the following prayer:

Lord, I believe in my heart that Jesus Christ is the Son of God. I believe that He was crucified to pay the price for my sins, and He was raised from the dead, that I might walk in newness of life. I confess Him now as my Lord. Jesus, please come into my heart and my life and forgive me of my sins and make me new. I thank You, Jesus, that You are now my Lord, and I am saved! I am a new creation in Christ. Old things have passed away and all things are made new!

SELF-CONTROL / TEMPTATION

I deny ungodliness and worldly lusts so that I may live soberly, righteously, and godly in this present world. [Titus 2:12]

I discipline my body like an athlete, training it to do what it should. [1 Corinthians 9:27]

Because I through the power of the Spirit put to death the deeds of my sinful nature, I will walk in life. [Romans 8:13]

The Word says that he that has no self-control is like a city that is broken down and without walls. Therefore I will walk in self-control and will rule over my own body rather than it ruling over me. [Proverbs 25:28]

I will "put on" the Lord Jesus Christ and make no provision for the flesh. [Romans 13:14]

The Word says that as many as are led by the Spirit of God, they are the sons of God. I declare that I will walk as a son, led by the Spirit of God. [Romans 8:14]

Self-control is a fruit of the Spirit. I have the Holy Spirit living in me; therefore, I have self-control. [Galatians 5:22]

The Lord delivers me out of all my temptations. [2 Peter 2:9]

The temptations in my life are no different than what others experience. But God is faithful and will not allow the temptation to be more than I can stand. When I am tempted, He provides me a way of escape. [1 Corinthians 10:13]

I am blessed because I am patient under trials and stand up under temptation. When I have stood the test and been approved, I will receive the victor's crown of life which God has promised to those who love Him. [James 1:12]

I have the grace that is in Christ Jesus to withstand every temptation. [2 Timothy 2:1]

When I am tempted, I will come boldly to the throne of grace and obtain mercy and find grace to help me in time of temptation. [Hebrews 4:16]

Because the Lord Himself suffered in being tempted, He is able to hear my cry and run to assist me when I am being tempted. [Hebrews 2:18]

The Lord Jesus is able to keep me from stumbling or slipping or falling, and He will present me faultless before the presence of His glory with exceeding joy. [Jude 1:24–25]

Because I am submitted to God, I resist the devil and he flees from me. [James 4:7]

I have hidden God's Word in my heart, and because His Word is hidden in me, I will not yield to temptation. [Psalm 119:11]

I seek, inquire for the Lord, and crave Him and His strength (His might and inflexibility to temptation); I seek and require His face and His presence forevermore. [Psalm 105:4]

In the day that I call, He answers me and He strengthens me with strength in my soul. [Psalm 138:3]

I will keep awake and watch and pray so that I will not fall into temptation. [Matthew 26:41]

I deny ungodliness and worldly lusts so that I may live a sober, righteous, and godly life. I discipline my body like an athlete, training it to do what it should. I walk in self-control and rule over my own body rather than it ruling over me. The Lord always provides me a way of escape from every temptation. The Lord Jesus is able to keep me from stumbling or slipping or falling. I have the grace that is in Christ Jesus to withstand every temptation. In the day that I call, He answers me and He strengthens me with strength (might and inflexibility to temptation) in my soul. Because I live a Spirit-filled, Spirit-led life, I am no longer controlled by substances or people or circumstances.

STRENGTH

I am strong in the Lord and in the power of His might. [Ephesians 6:10]

I have strength for all things in Christ who empowers me. I am ready for anything and equal to anything through Him who infuses inner strength into me; I am self-sufficient in Christ's sufficiency. [Philippians 4:13]

The Lord gives me strength when I am weak and power when I feel powerless. [Isaiah 40:29]

I will wait upon the Lord and be of good courage, and He will strengthen my heart. [Psalm 27:14]

The Lord gives strength to me and He blesses me with peace. [Psalm 29:11]

Because I wait upon the Lord (expect, look for, and hope in Him), I am being renewed in my strength. I will mount up with wings as eagles; I will run and not be weary; I will walk and not faint. [Isaiah 40:31]

My flesh and my heart may fail, but God is the strength of my heart. He is mine forever. [Psalm 73:26]

In returning to the Lord and resting in Him, I am saved. In quietness and confidence is my strength. [Isaiah 30:15]

The Lord will grant me out of the rich treasury of His glory to be strengthened in my inner man through His Spirit which dwells in me. [Ephesians 3:16]

I will be strong in the grace that is in Christ Jesus. [2 Timothy 2:1]

The Lord is my strength and my shield. My heart trusts in Him and I am helped. Therefore, my heart greatly rejoices, and with my song I will praise Him. [Psalm 28:7]

I am strong in the Lord and in the power of His might. I have strength for all things in Christ who empowers me. I am ready for anything and equal to anything through Him who infuses inner strength into me. Because I wait upon the Lord (expect, look for, and hope in Him), I am being renewed in my strength. I will mount up with wings as eagles; I will run and not be weary; I will walk and not faint. God is the strength of my heart. The Lord gives me strength when I am weak and power when I am powerless.

TRUST

I trust in the Lord with my whole heart and do not lean on my own understanding. I acknowledge Him in all my ways, and He directs my paths. [Proverbs 3:5–6]

I commit my ways to the Lord and trust in Him. [Psalm 37:5]

The Lord is my rock and my fortress and my deliverer. He is my God and my strength. In Him I will trust. [Psalm 18:2]

Because I trust in the Lord, I can rejoice. I will ever shout for joy because He defends me. [Psalm 5:11]

I praise God for His Word. I trust in Him, so why should I be afraid? What can mere mortals do to me? [Psalm 56:4]

I trust in my God at all times. I pour out my heart before Him. He is my refuge and my protection. [Psalm 62:8]

The Lord is a shield to me because of my trust in Him. [Psalm 18:30]

Because I trust in the Lord, I am like Mount Zion which cannot be shaken or moved. [Psalm 125:1]

God is my salvation. I will trust in Him, and I will not be afraid. The Lord is my strength and my song. He has given me the victory. [Isaiah 12:2]

God is the God of my strength in whom I will trust. He is my shield and the horn of my salvation. He is my

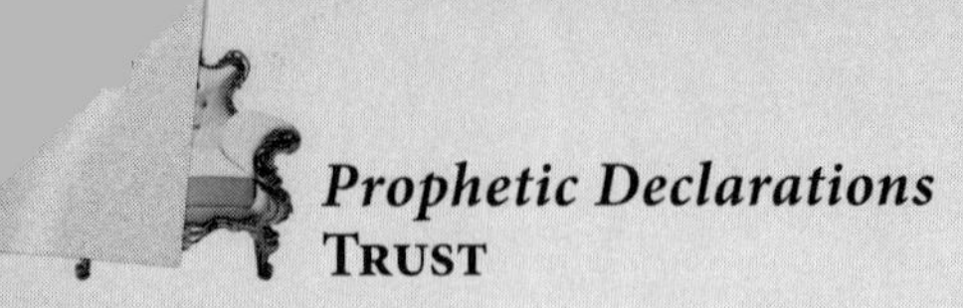

stronghold and my refuge, my Savior who saves me from violence. [2 Samuel 22:3]

I am blessed because I put my trust in my God. [Psalm 2:12]

God is a shield to me because I trust in Him. [2 Samuel 22:31]

I trust in the Lord with my whole heart and do not lean on my own understanding. I commit my ways to the Lord and trust in Him. Because of my trust in the Lord, He is a shield to me. Because I trust in the Lord, I can rejoice, and I will ever shout for joy because He defends me. I will trust in Him, and I will not be afraid. Because I trust in the Lord, I am like Mount Zion which cannot be shaken or moved!

VICTORY

In all things, I am more than a conqueror through Jesus who loves me. [Romans 8:37]

I thank my God who always causes me to triumph in Christ. [2 Corinthians 2:14]

In Christ, God leads me from place to place in one perpetual victory parade. [2 Corinthians 2:14]

In this world, I may have tribulation, but I will be of good cheer because Jesus has overcome the world. [John 16:33]

I overcome by the Blood of the Lamb and by the Word of my testimony. [Revelation 12:11]

I sing unto the Lord, for He has done marvelous things. His right hand and His holy arm have gotten Him the victory, and therefore I have the victory. [Psalm 98:1]

Lord, Yours is the greatness and the power and the glory and the victory and the majesty. All that is in the Heaven and in the earth is Yours. Yours is the Kingdom, O Lord, and You are exalted as head above all. [1 Chronicles 29:11]

Lord, You have made me glad through Your works. I will triumph in the works of Your hands. [Psalm 92:4]

If God be for me, who can be against me? [Romans 8:31]

I declare that no weapon formed against me will prosper! [Isaiah 54:17]

Greater is He that is in me than he that is in the world. [1 John 4:4]

I am more than a conqueror through Jesus who loves me. My God always causes me to triumph in Christ. Greater is He that is in me than he that is in the world! If God be for me, who can be against me? I sing unto the Lord, for He has done marvelous things. His right hand and His holy arm have gotten Him the victory, and therefore I have the victory! In Christ, God leads me from place to place in one perpetual victory parade!

WISDOM

When I need wisdom, I ask God who gives to all men liberally, and wisdom is given to me. [James 1:5]

The Lord gives me the Spirit of wisdom and revelation in the knowledge of Him. [Ephesians 1:17]

I am of Christ Jesus who is made unto me wisdom and righteousness and sanctification and redemption. [1 Corinthians 1:30]

Lord, Your wisdom and understanding is better than gold and silver! [Proverbs 16:16]

The Lord gives me wisdom. Out of His mouth comes knowledge and understanding to me. [Proverbs 2:5–6]

The Spirit of the Lord rests upon me, the Spirit of wisdom and understanding, the Spirit of counsel and might, the Spirit of knowledge and of the fear of the Lord. [Isaiah 11:2]

Because I am righteous, my mouth utters wisdom and my tongue speaks what is just. [Psalm 37:30]

My mouth speaks words of wisdom and my heart is filled with insight. [Psalm 49:3]

The Lord makes me to know wisdom in my inmost heart. [Psalm 51:6]

The fear of the Lord is the foundation of wisdom in me. Because I obey His commands, I grow in wisdom. [Psalm 111:10]

The Lord grants wisdom to me. From His mouth come knowledge and understanding. He stores up sound wisdom for me. [Proverbs 2:6]

Because I find wisdom and gain understanding, I am happy and blessed. [Proverbs 3:13]

I pay attention to God's wisdom. I listen to His wise counsel. [Proverbs 5:1]

I gain wisdom because wisdom is the principal thing. [Proverbs 4:7]

I pay attention to God's wisdom. I listen to His wise counsel. From the Lord's mouth come knowledge and understanding. He stores up sound wisdom for me. When I need wisdom, I ask God who gives to me liberally. I am of Christ Jesus who is made unto me wisdom. The Spirit of the Lord rests upon me, the Spirit of wisdom and understanding. My mouth speaks words of wisdom and my heart is filled with insight. The Lord places me on paths of wisdom and keeps me walking in them all the days of my life.

WORD (THE WORD OF GOD)

The Word of God is a lamp to my feet (showing me where I am) and a light to my path (showing me where I am going). [Psalm 119:105]

I rejoice in the Word of God as one that finds great treasure. [Psalm 119:162]

The words of the Lord are perfect; they revive my soul. His words are trustworthy; they make me wise. His words are right; they bring joy to my heart. His words are clear; they give me insight for living. The words of the Lord are more desirable than the finest gold. They are sweeter than honey. [Psalm 19:7–10]

The Word of God is quick and powerful, sharper than any two-edged sword. It severs every cord of wickedness and affliction from my life and sets me free from every bond of the enemy. [Hebrews 4:12]

God's Word has revived me and given me life. [Psalm 119:50]

I obey God's Word. I cleanse my way and make it pure by taking heed to God's Word. [Psalm 119:9]

God's Word is like a fire that consumes every obstacle or problem in my life. It is like a hammer that breaks in pieces the rock of most stubborn resistance. [Jeremiah 23:29]

God's Word is life to me and health to all my flesh. [Proverbs 4:22]

When I speak God's Word, it accomplishes, it produces. [Isaiah 55:11]

God upholds me according to His Word, that I may live. [Psalm 119:116]

God gives me understanding so that I may keep His Word and obey it with all my heart. [Psalm 119:34]

God's Word is forever settled in Heaven, and it is forever settled in me. [Psalm 119:89]

God's promises come to pass for me according to His Word. [Luke 1:38]

When I speak God's Word, He is listening and watching to see that His Word is fulfilled. [Jeremiah 1:12]

I am a doer of God's Word, not a hearer only. [James 1:22]

When I speak God's Word, it does not return void but it accomplishes and it produces. [Isaiah 55:11]

God has magnified His Word above His Name, and I allow His Word to be magnified in my life and above every situation and circumstance. [Psalm 138:2]

The Word of God is a lamp to my feet (showing me where I am) and a light to my path (showing me where I am going). God's Word is like a fire that consumes every obstacle or problem in my life. It is like a hammer that breaks in pieces the rock of most stubborn resistance. God's Word is life to me and health to all my flesh. When I speak God's Word, it accomplishes, it produces. God has magnified His Word above His Name, and I allow His Word to be magnified in my life and above every circumstance. His words are perfect, trustworthy, right, and clear. His words revive my soul, make me wise, give me insight for living, and bring joy to my heart. I rejoice in the Word of God as one that finds great treasure. His words are more desirable to me than the finest gold, and they are sweeter than honey!

ABOUT THE AUTHOR

DR. SANDRA G. KENNEDY is the founder and president of Sandra Kennedy Ministries®, as well as founder and senior pastor of Whole Life Ministries® in Augusta, Georgia. A highly sought after speaker, Dr. Kennedy travels and ministers extensively throughout the world teaching at conferences, seminars and churches. She has a local, national and international television ministry. Her passion is to fulfill her God-given mandate to "Grow up the body of Christ and teach them victory."

CONTACT THE AUTHOR

Sandra Kennedy Ministries

2621 Washington Rd.

Augusta, GA 30904

706-737-4530

www.SandraKennedy.org